Of Loss, Grief and Hope

The Journey of the Sibling, the Mother and the Child who went to heaven

Written and Illustrated by
Kristina Sanchez-Mills

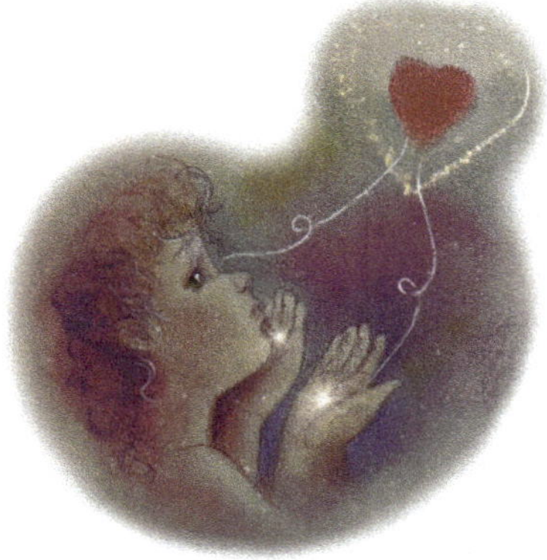

Waldenhouse Publishers, Inc.
Walden, Tennessee

Of Loss, Grief, and Hope: The Journey of the Sibling, the Mother and the Child who went to heaven

Illustrated by Kristina Sanchez-Mills
Type and design by Karen Paul Stone
Published by Waldenhouse Publishers, Inc.
100 Clegg Street, Signal Mountain, Tennessee 37377 USA
423-886-2721 www.waldenhouse.com
Printed in the United States of America
ISBN: 978-1-947589-68-1 hardcover
ISBN: 978-1-947589-70-4 softcover
Library of Congress Control Number: 2023930285
A mother lays bare three perspectives framed in art and words that shed light upon the loss of a child. - Provided by publisher
FAM014000 FAMILY & RELATIONSHIPS / Death, Grief, Bereavement
REL012010 RELIGION / Christian Living / Death, Grief, Bereavement
ART050000 ART / Subjects & Themes / General

To my beloved daughters Ariadna and Rosalia

I thought I knew about love until I had you; then, I discovered I had not scratched the surface! Your love forever changed me. It made me a better version of myself.

In my life, you are my biggest accomplishment!

I am so proud to be your mami.

Forever and a day, I will love you!

Kristina

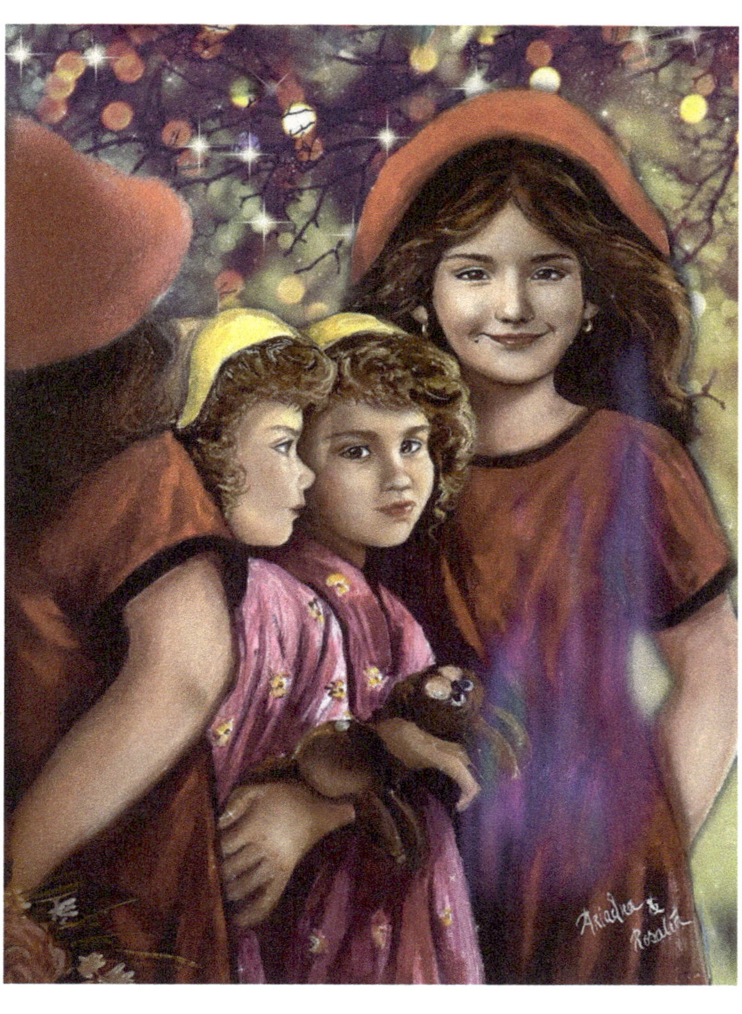

Acknowledgments

I thank God for depositing these books into my spirit and for being the force that sustained me during the cathartic and, at times, painful process of telling our story. You imparted huge lessons that I shall carry in my spirit forever.

I want to thank my dear friend, John H. McCreedy, for being by my side since day one. Thank you for believing in me. For giving me your support in every way possible – even if by doing so, the pain of losing your own child could be triggered. What a process this has been for both of us! I am so blessed to have you in my life!

I want to offer my gratitude to both my beloved daughter Rosalia A. York and my husband Kevin J. Mills for supporting me and believing in me. They both know the big deal these books represent in my life. Kevin, thank you for putting up with my roller coaster of emotions and not running for the door!

Rosie, thank you for being the voice to remind me this is the project God wanted me to do, if I were awarded the grant. I know your part in this book has awakened a lot of painful feelings. I pray it brings healing as well.

Thank you, to Nicole Chandler, to Jane Kaplan, to my therapist Leslie Davis, to Jayden Watkins and to all of my friends, clients and students that one way or another have supported it me in this journey.

It takes a village!

"It is not the length of life, but depth of life"

Ralph Waldo Emerson

Introduction

18 years ago, I went through the most terrible loss a parent can experience.

I lost my oldest child.

The loss was due to a battle with childhood cancer that ended up in the ultimate loss. Our lives changed forever!

The journey has been a very difficult one. I have walked a path of darkness that sometimes has been dotted by speckles of light. Often times darkness has inundated the entire trail. There have been waves of excruciating pain, peace, brokenness, madness ... healing and more hope.

About 10 years or so ago, God planted a dream in my heart: "Write your story." I argued, "But how I am going to pay for it?" In my spirit I would hear, "Just write your story." It was a beautiful dream, yet, one I thought almost impossible because of the cost involved. Until my miracle came in late 2021: A grant from *Artsbuild* in Chattanooga, was bestowed upon me to make the dream a reality! I cannot thank God enough! I am so grateful to this organization and the private sponsors that provided the funding for this limited first edition.

The notion of our story evolved into a one very clear idea. I was to write about our experience from three different perspectives:

- Rosalia "Rosie," my surviving child: *The Sibling's Journey*
  An account of the story from the standpoint of the young sibling. A journal about her experiences and the impacts that the whole thing has had in her young life.
- My own experience as the mother: *The Mother's Journey*
  A medley of thoughts, learnings, poetry and accounts of some of the supernatural experiences I have had over time concerning this loss.
- The story from Ariadna "Ari," my older child's point of view: *The Child Who Went to Heaven.* To my surprise her account of the events begins with her death.

My deepest desire is that our story impacts – in a positive manner – the individuals touched directly by the loss of a child or a loved one. I hope that our journey can be a mirror of source, in which you can find validation of your own feelings. I pray with all of my heart that in your own journey, you will find the strength to continue your path into healing, peace and hope.

I feel that this story can also benefit people that aren't directly impacted by the loss. As a "caring outsider" you might be able to gain a better understanding of the impact of the situation and the repercussions in many areas of the affected individual's life. It was impossible to account for every single facet affected. I shared what I felt were the most relevant. Although the financial repercussions can be devastating, I did not go there in this book. As you learn of the struggles and the murky nature of grief, my hope is that your empathy and compassion will grow and be transformed so you can offer better support to the bereaved in your life. My prayer is that God does something beyond powerful with this dream that – thanks to Him – is now a reality!

Foreword

The creator of this beautiful book draws the reader into a world where a family's inner strength, deep faith, and unconditional love come face-to-face with the unimaginable loss of a child.

The artist's trilogy captures the incredible strength of an innocent child, the confusion of a loving sibling, and the unrelenting perseverance of a mother striving to find meaning where, some may argue, there is none to be found.

But that is a fallacy, and Ms. Sanchez-Mills proves it in a way that will ease the pain, soothe the heart, and uplift the soul of those who have found themselves on the threshold of absolute despair.

John H. McCreedy

Contents

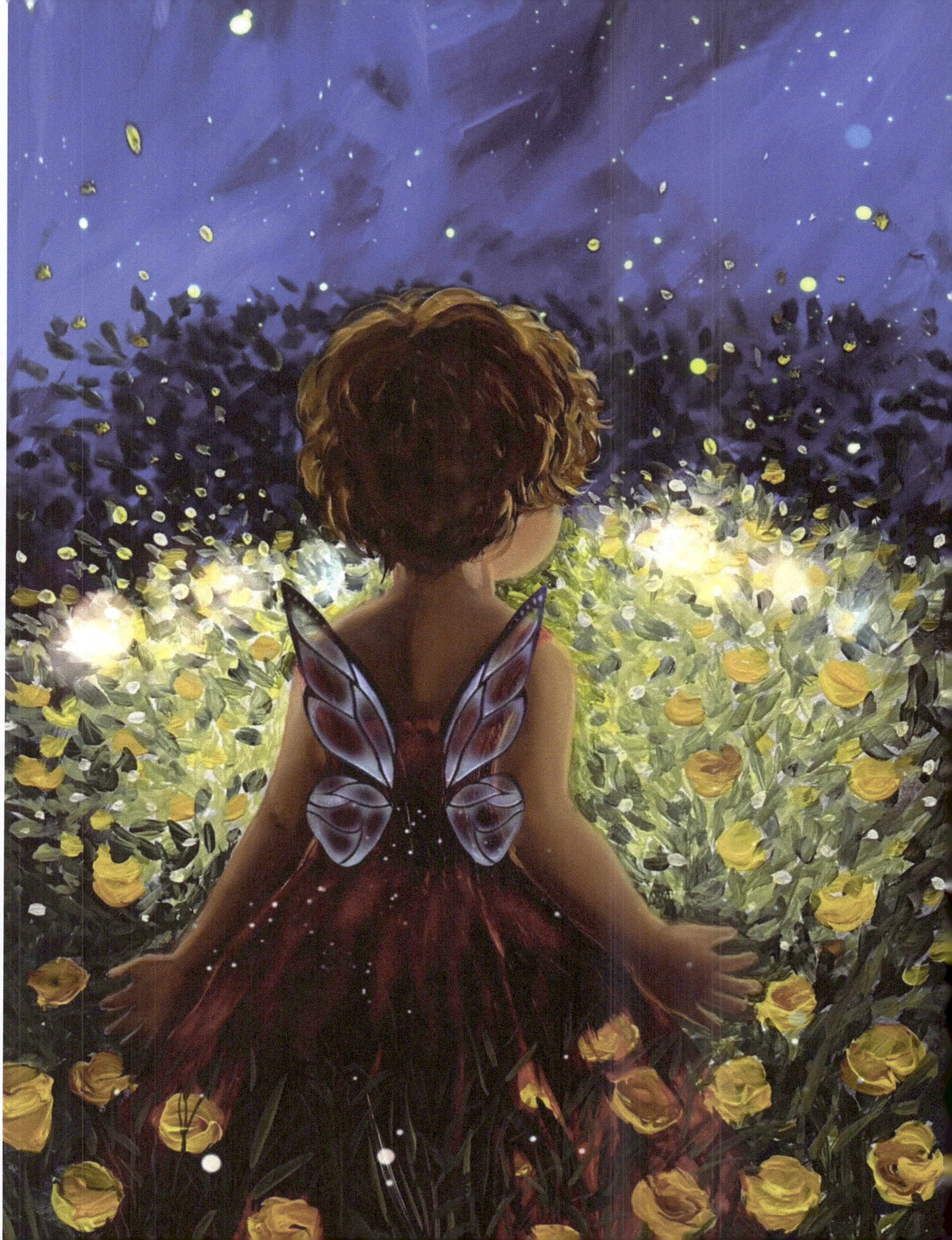

The Little Sister's Journey

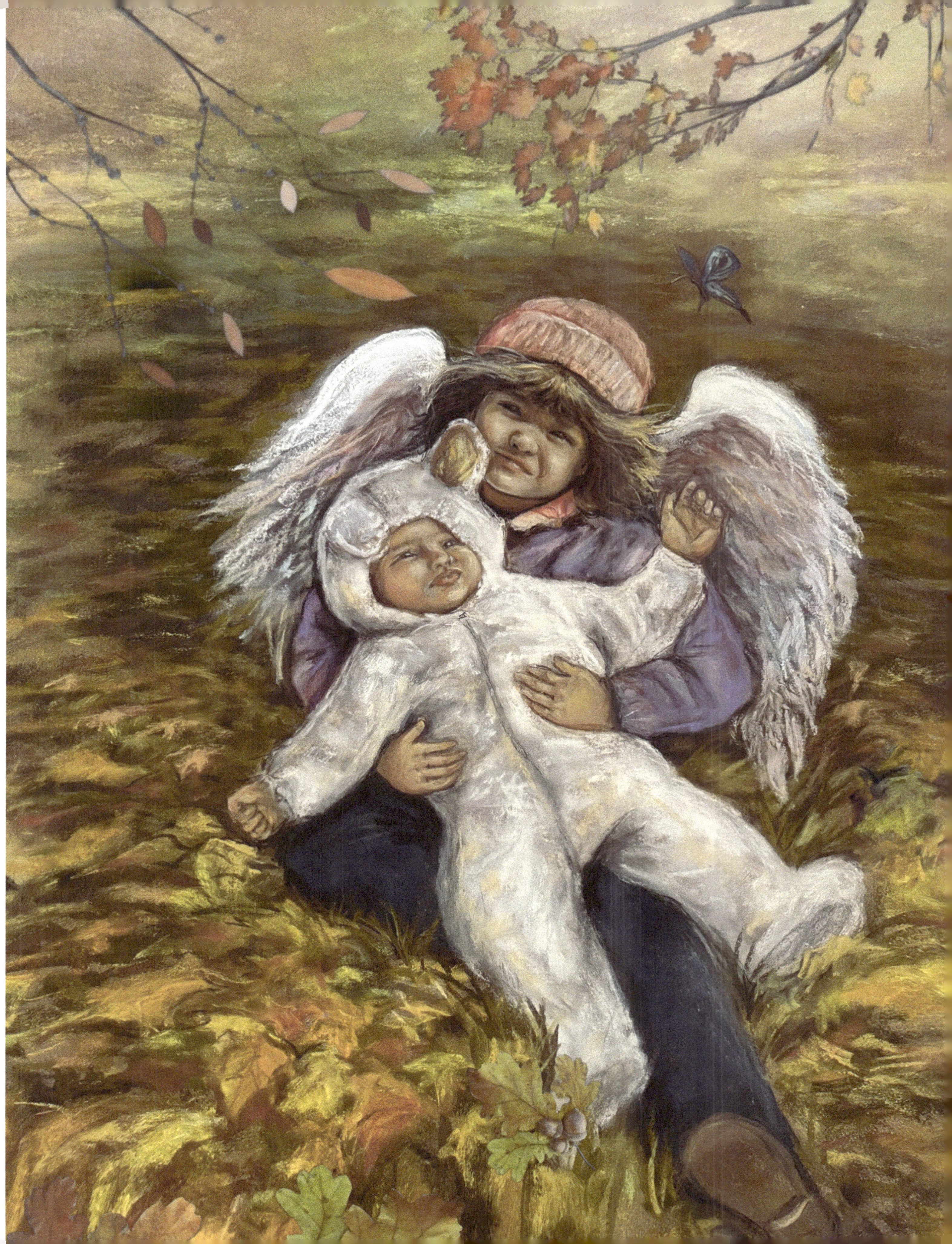

Part One

My big sister Ari was three years old when I was born. Ever since then, we have been inseparable. She even helped my mom take care of me when I was a baby! I love her so much!

Ari teaches me that all things are possible when we are together. She shares even her most secret stories from her imagination with me.

We share days full of adventures as we play make believe and dress up. Sometimes she is a mighty queen and I, a princess or even her servant; but I don't mind that at all.

Other times we are animals of the jungle or magical creatures that take flight day and night.

We also love to find enchanted spots outside in our backyard to go camping and exploring. Most times we find little critters that we take as pets, but don't tell Mom; she doesn't know!

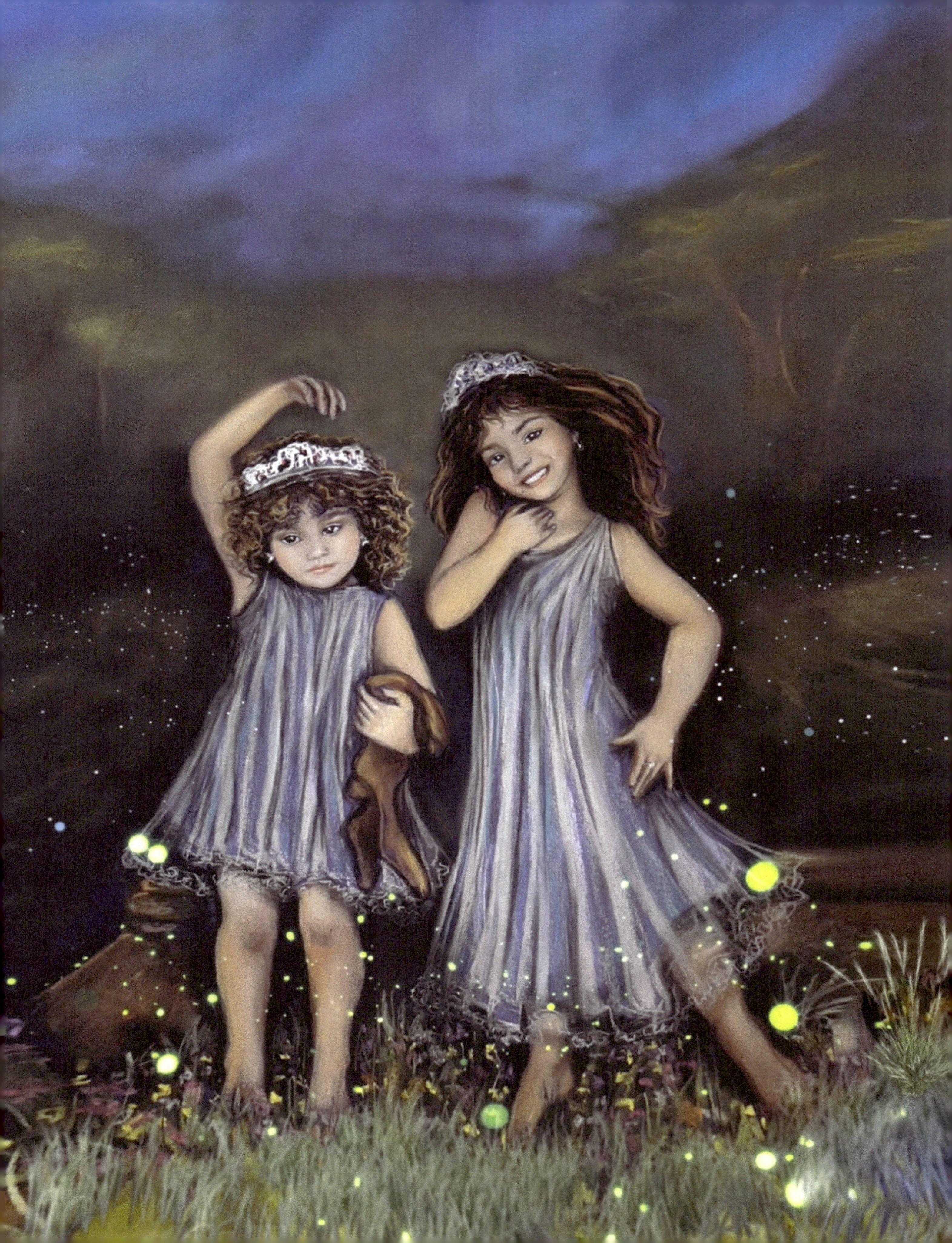

My big sister is my teacher and sometimes my defender. She doesn't always tell on me when I mess up, to keep me out of trouble.

She knows me so well. She knows when I am smiling – even if it's dark and she can't see me!

Other times, my sister is the reason I'm not smiling. Sometimes she can be unkind to me. And I can be mean to her, too. But even so, we still love each other very much.

We love each other when we are at our best and when we are at our worst.

This is our life. Until one day, everything changes.

It's a sunny afternoon and we have just come home from school. I try to convince Ari to come outside with me to play hide and seek, our favorite game. But she says she is too tired. She doesn't even want to watch a movie!

The next day, she doesn't want to get up from bed. She stays home from school. When I come home, I want to tell her about my day, but she only wants to sleep.

These weird days are followed by many more.

Now, she doesn't play as much with me, and I feel sad and lonely.

What is happening to my sister? I just don't understand. Why does she not want to spend time with me any longer?

"Ari, are you mad at me? Please don't be mad at me!"

"Rose, I am not mad at you, I promise. I just don't feel good enough to play. But I can read you a story if you lie down next to me," she says.

I hop in bed with her, but four pages into the story she falls asleep!

I tell Mom about it.

"Rose, you need to be patient with your big sister. She is sick, but we are giving her medicine. She will be well soon enough, you'll see."

I go outside to pick flowers for Ari. I know they will make her feel better!

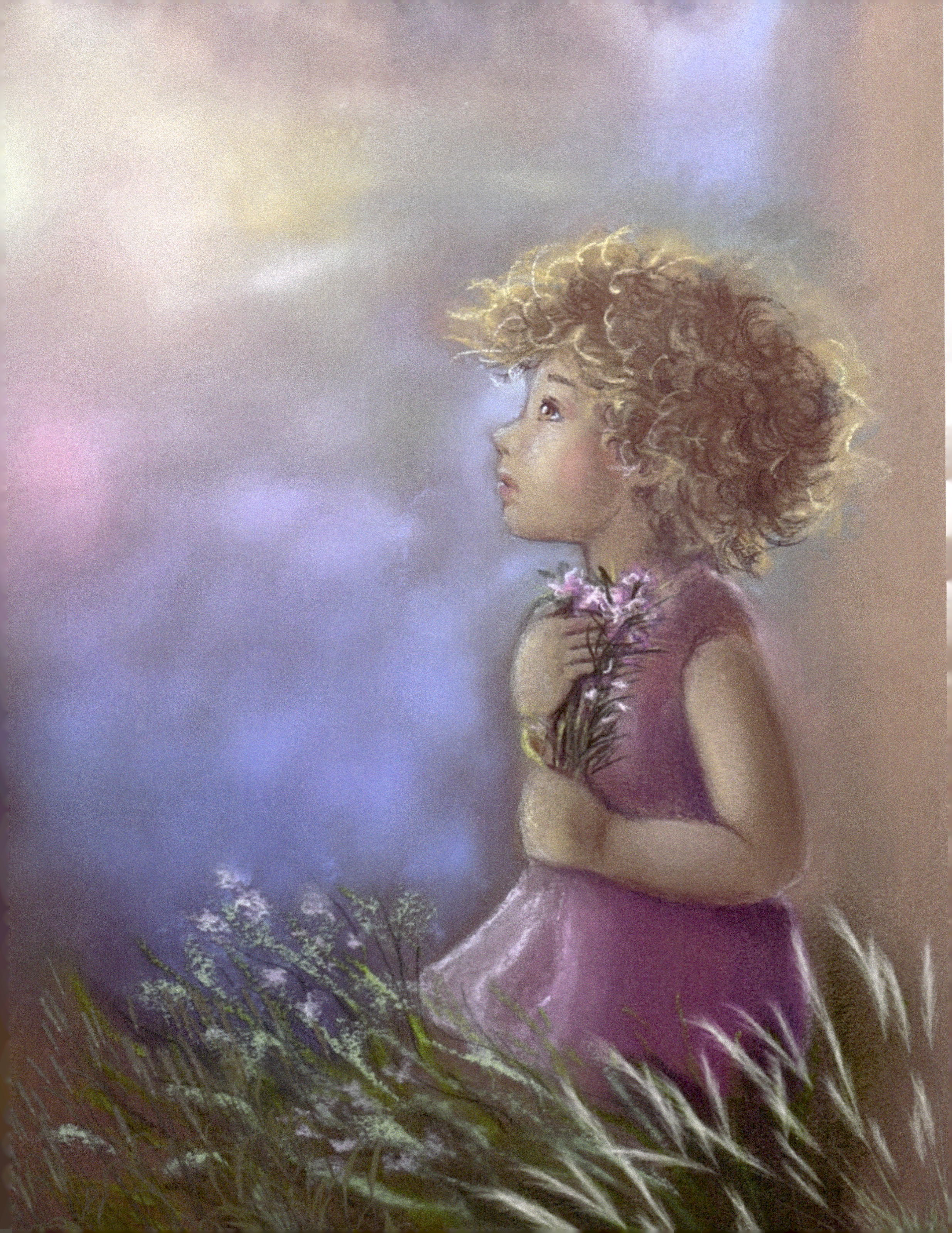

Many more days go by. We barely play now because Ari is still not feeling well. We have been to the clinic so many times that I've lost count.

Now, we are going to see a different doctor at a hospital. As we go out, my sister holds my hand and I ask her, "Do you love me again?"

"Silly Rose! I have never stopped loving you, not for a moment!"

I feel so happy!!!

Can I tell you something? I hate going to the hospital. Ugh! But I will go every day if it makes Ari OK again.

My sister is feeling better today!

The play room in the new hospital is so cool! They have all kinds of games and toys! I guess I don't hate this hospital after all.

We get to play while Mom and Dad are talking to the doctors. Yay!!!

Tonight, my sister is extra tired from playing so much, so I tell her a made-up bedtime story and she loves it. I sleep right beside my sister and my bunny all night and have many happy dreams.

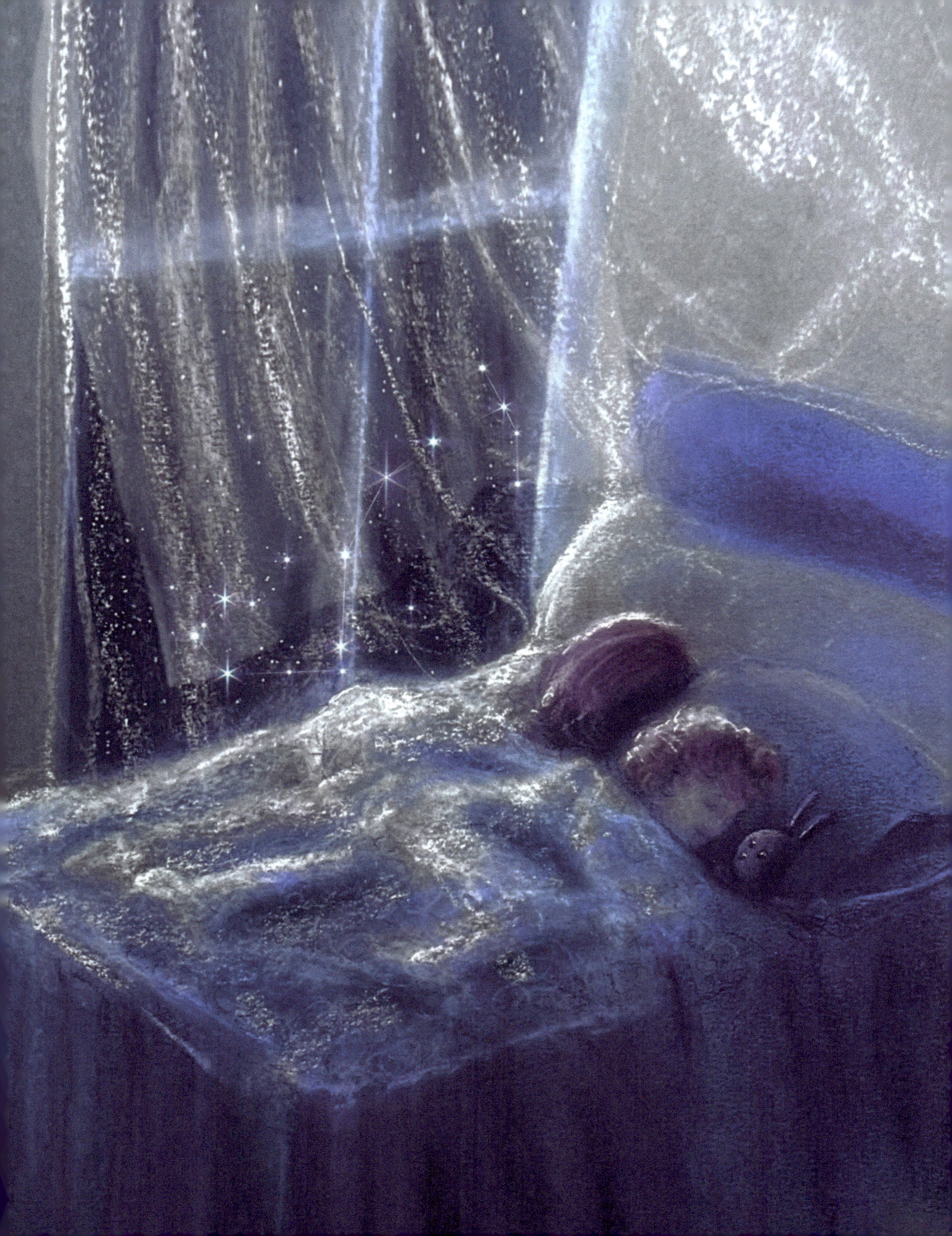

Today we are skipping school. We are going back to the new hospital and I'm excited! I get to play in the cool play room again!! The only thing is, my sister is sick today and doesn't want to play with me this time.

Mom and Dad are very serious. Are they mad at me? I think I have been a good girl, but did I do something wrong?

Mom is crying and Dad is rubbing his head a lot. My sister is inside that room with the nurses. I have a weird feeling in my chest. I'm scared.

I remind my mom that the doctors can give my sister more medicine and that she will be fine. My Mom looks at me with her big shiny eyes and then she hugs me and smiles a little crooked smile.

I love it when my mom hugs me, only this time it feels different. I think I feel sadness in her.

I tell my mom, "I will protect my sister, Mom. Don't you worry about her."

Today I hear Dad talking on the phone with Grandpa. He sounds frightened. He says words I don't understand – something about my sister having cancer? I don't know what cancer is, but I am frightened, too.

Is Ari going to be OK? Did she get cancer because I have been mad at her for not playing with me?

I run to my sister's bedroom. I want to rub her legs like I do when she says they hurt. She usually likes that, but this time she says no.

"I don't feel good, Rose," she says. "Everything hurts."

"You will feel better tomorrow – you'll see," I tell her.

But many tomorrows come and go and still she does not feel better.

She stays sick no matter what I try. I just don't know what I'm supposed to do.

I feel terribly bad for her.

I feel like crying, but for some reason I can't.

I think I need to be strong, but I don't know how.

After dinner my dad tells my sister and me a good night story, one of our favorite tales! After he is finished, I stay and sing a lullaby to my big sister. She falls asleep with a grin on her lovely face!

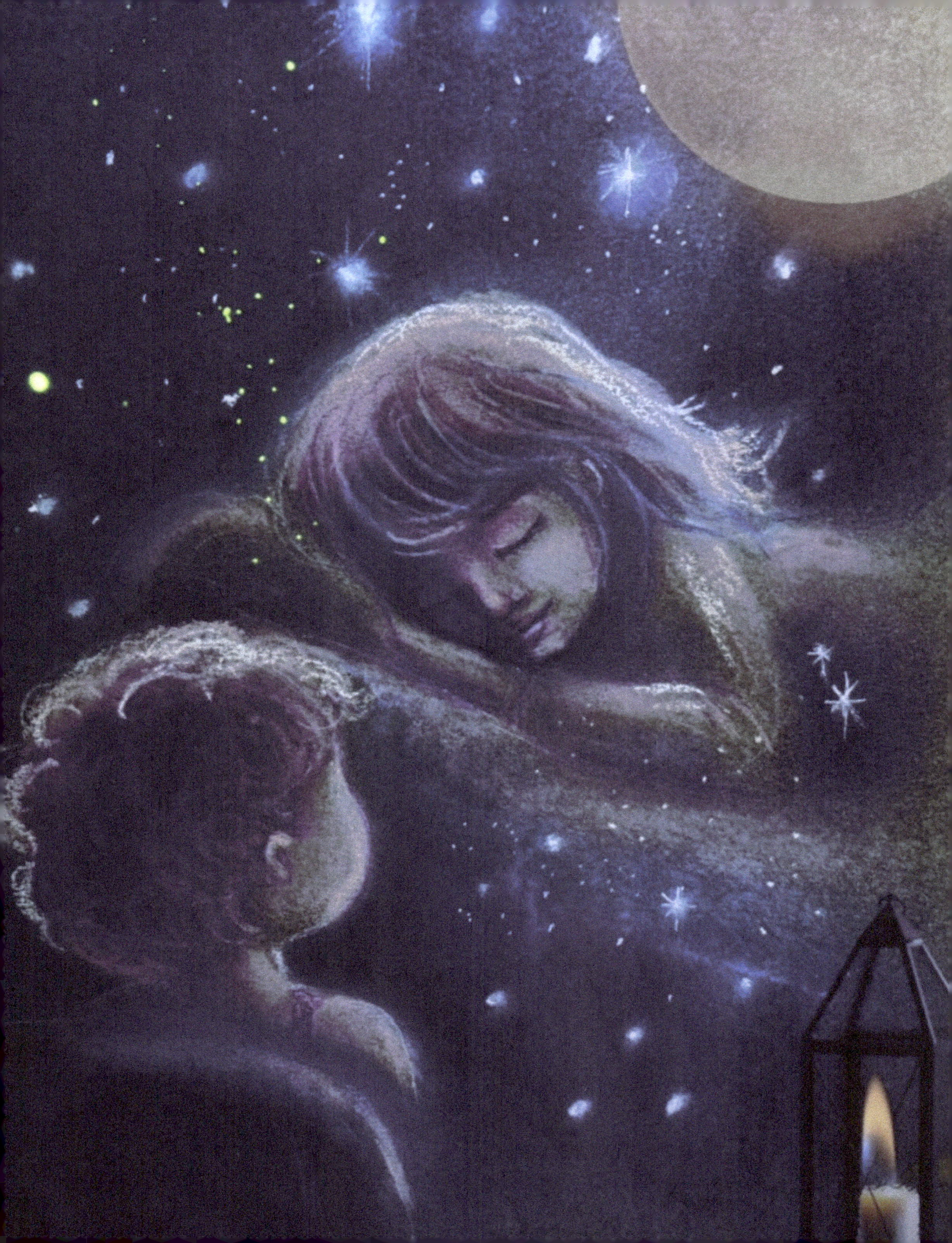

Today we are going back to the hospital. My parents tell me they are going to give her a medicine called chemotherapy to make her well again. I am so happy!

Hey, cancer, you are getting out of my sister's body!!

But after they give her the chemotherapy medicine, Ari becomes very ill, and I am scared!

Daddy comes and takes me for a walk. He says that chemotherapy sometimes makes people vomit. He says it's normal, and it means the medicine is working.

"Honey Bunny, your sister is going to be OK," he says. "The next few days are going to be difficult – she might feel sicker before she gets better. We just have to trust that she will be well again. We have to be strong for her. You can be strong for her, right, Monkey Head?"

And I say I can.

Months go by and they keep giving Ari more and more chemotherapy. It still makes her very sick.

Today, I brush her hair and it is falling out! A lot! My parents tell us she will lose all of her hair. Ari is very sad and I am sad too. I'm going to give her my doll's wig. It's made of pretty shiny hair just like hers used to be.

I see the nurses, how they care for my sister. I decide to be her nurse too! I think she likes it when I play nurse and tell her stories and do silly things to make her smile.

Before bed, she tells me, "I hate being sick. I miss school and my friends. But you know what? I am so happy you are my little sister. I love you, Rose!" And she hugs me and kisses me on the cheek.

My heart is soaring all the way up to the sky!

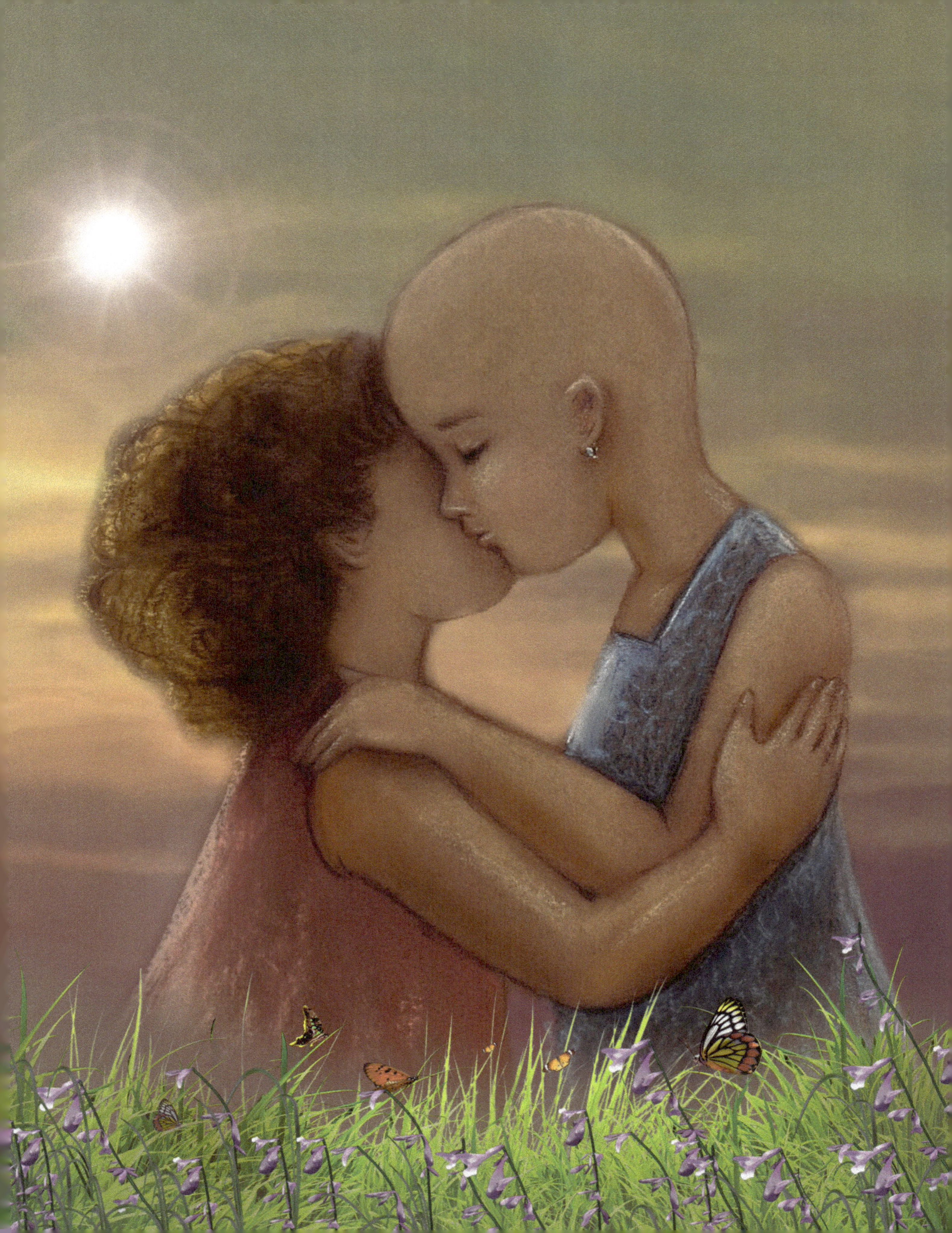

Today one of my mom's friends from work comes to pick me up from school. She tells me my parents had to take Ari to St. Jude Hospital. She takes me to her home and says I will stay with her family for a few days.

It's fun to be here. I get to play with my best friend!

But I feel sad too. I miss Ari, my mommy, my daddy and my home.

A few days later when they come back, Mom tells me Ari had to have a new treatment and I couldn't be in the hospital room while they did that. She says they missed me terribly! My sister hugs me and Papi says they love me very much.

I'm glad they are back, but I still don't understand what's happening. Why do they have to go away to that hospital? Why can't they take me?

That night after supper, my mommy tells us:

"My darlings, there is a very special cord made of three strings. Two of them are made of love and one is made of faith.

"There is a love that comes from outside. I think of it as God's love for us. Then there is the love that comes from within us. This is the love we have for one another. And the third string is faith – the kind of faith that believes even if we can't see, the kind of faith that believes in the impossible."

She says that because the cord is made that way, it is so strong, so powerful, that nothing can EVER break it!

"This cord keeps us connected even when we are away from each other. So, even when we have to be in different places, like in the hospital, at school, or anywhere at all, we are always, ALWAYS, together – always connected no matter what!"

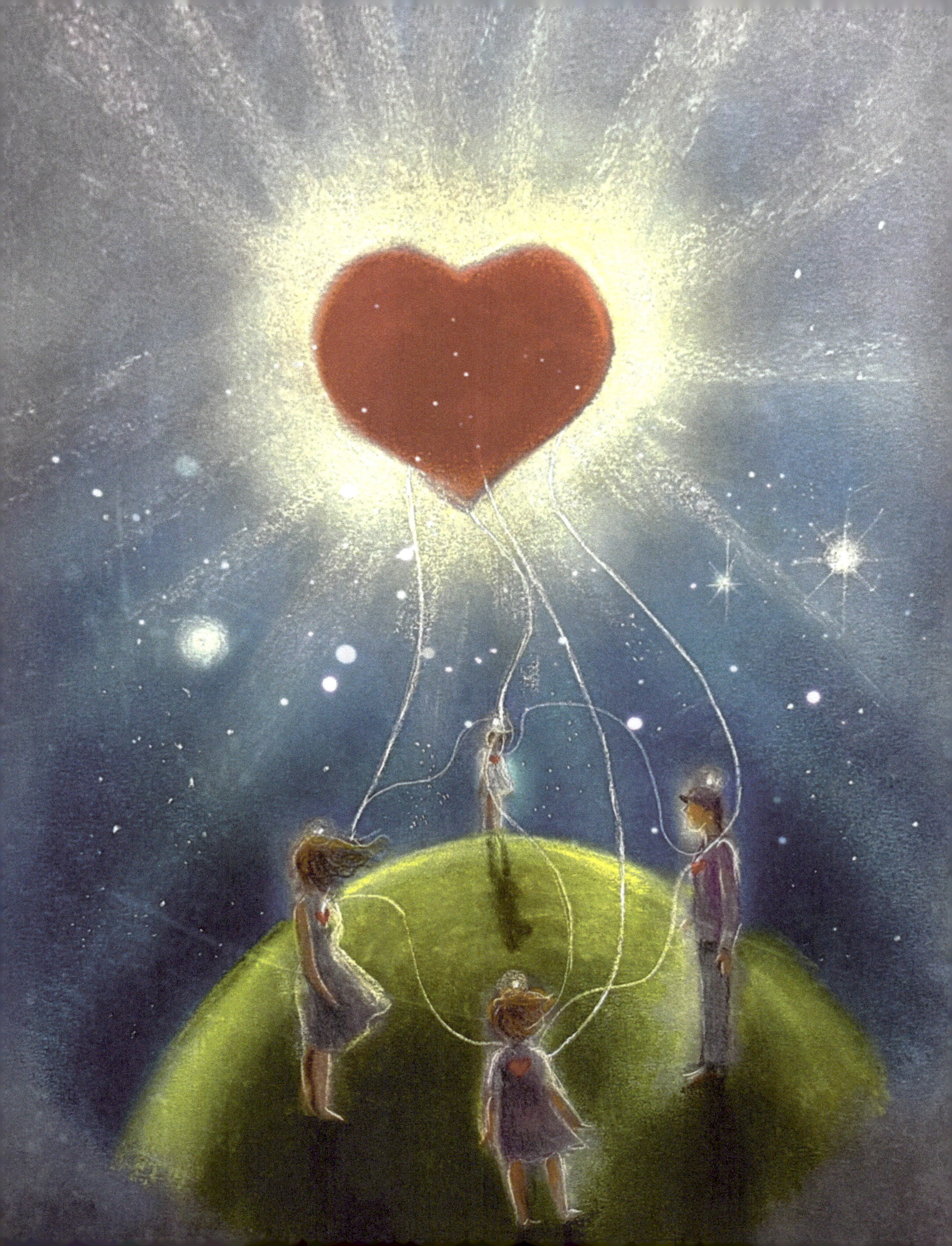

The next day at school some kids are making fun of my sister. They pull on her wig and make her cry! I'm not going to let anyone be cruel to Ari! I won't!

I am so mad, and I punch them hard.

Later my parents sit me down to talk. They say they understand why I felt so angry. "It is good to stand up to bullies, Monkey Bunny. But fighting is not the answer. We are going to talk to the teacher and the kids."

I'm not sure those unkind kids will listen!

But later that week, there is a big meeting with all the children and teachers in the school. My sister's nurse comes to help us talk to them. She and my mommy explain many things about my sister being sick, about cancer, about why she lost her hair.

I'm surprised that many of the kids, even those who were cruel to Ari, ask a lot of questions!

And guess what? After that day, no one makes fun of my sister again!

Many weeks pass, and now my sister and mom are traveling to St. Jude Hospital more often.

I feel very lonely at times. I try to keep myself busy with my drawings, my toys and my games. It helps to remember about the threefold cord that keeps us connected.

I also pray like my mommy taught me. I pray things will go back to the way they were before my sister got cancer.

I miss that time so much.

I just want us to be able to play together again.

I just want Ari to be well.

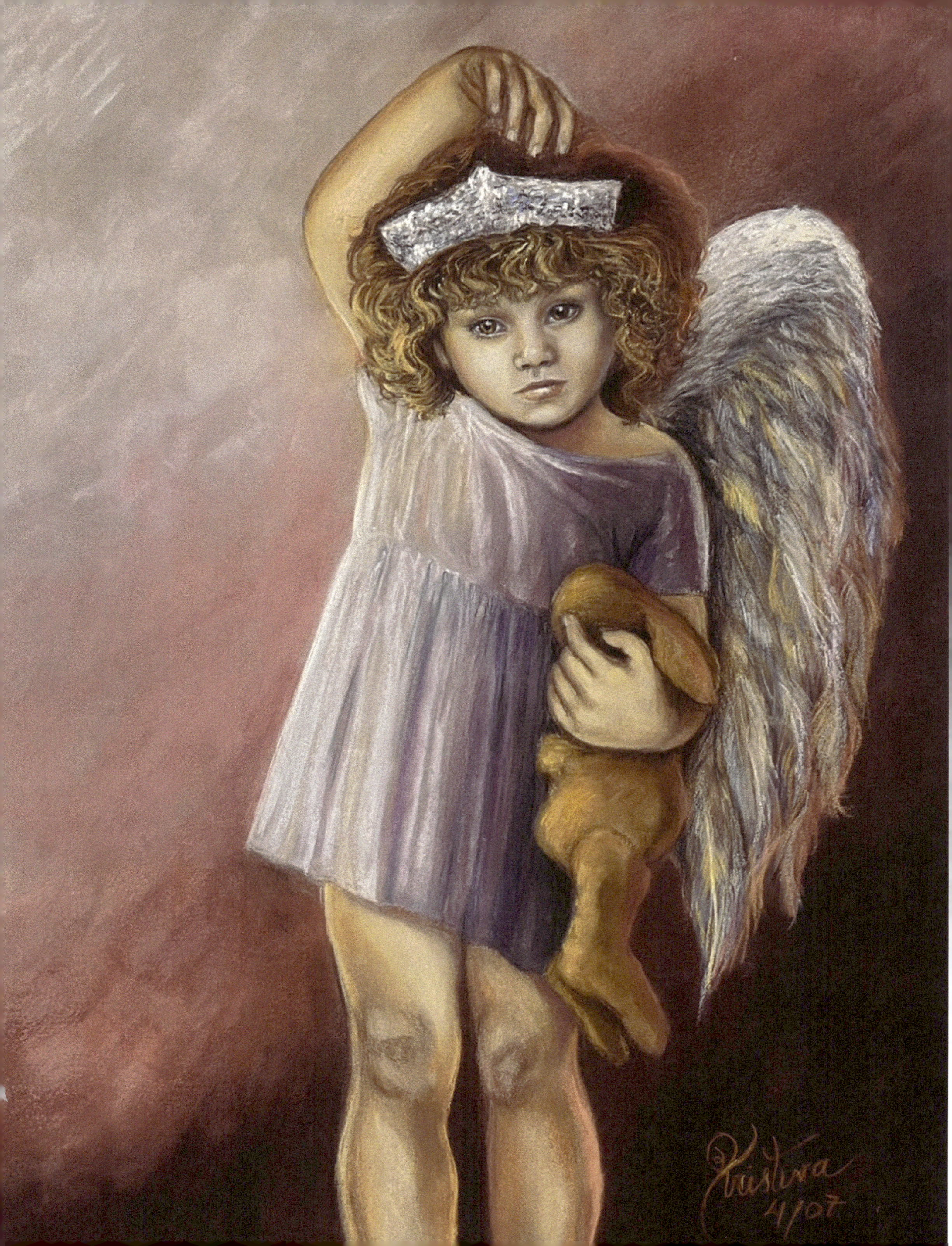

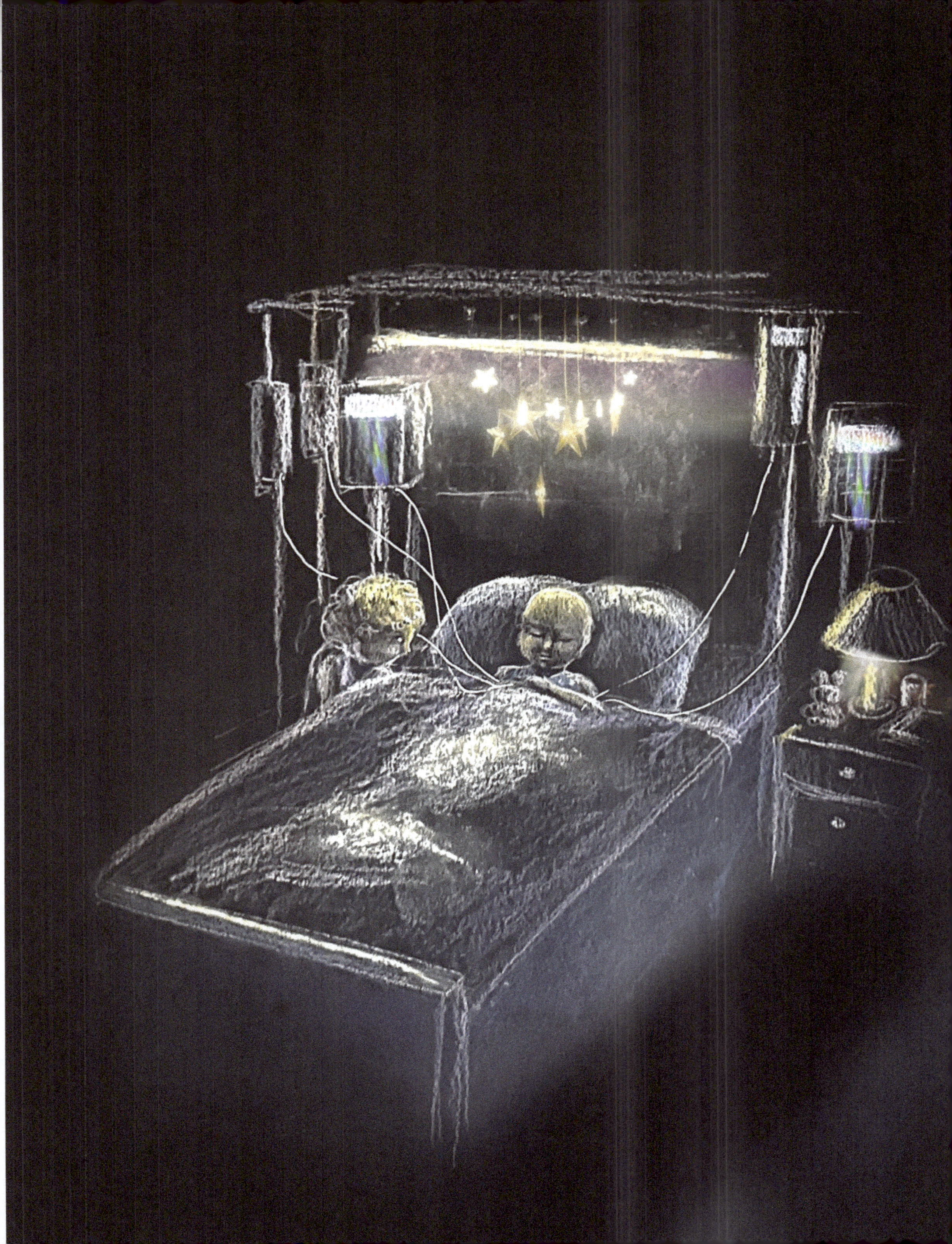

My sister has gotten sicker. I can see it, and it frightens me!

I hear my mama talking to Grandma on the phone. She and my aunt are coming to town to help. We are going back to St. Jude's but this time we will all go together!

When we arrive, they put my sister in a big room with strings that connect her to many loud machines. It is scary to see, and there is a strong medicine smell that makes me feel sick to my stomach.

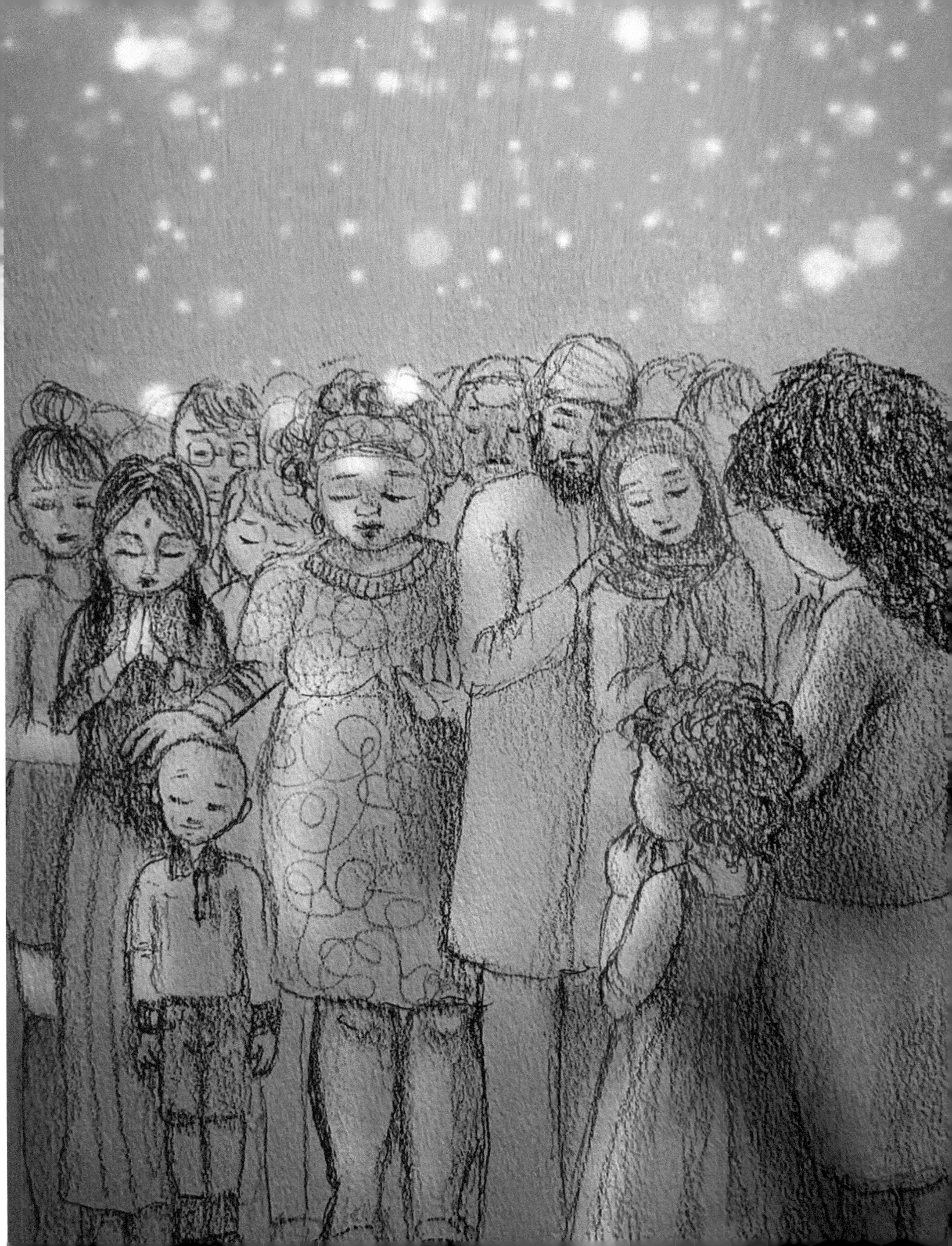

Later that day, I go with Grandma to stay at a place called Target House, which is a place for families who have a sick child at St. Jude's, like Ari.

For days, I go from Target House to the hospital and back. I can play with my sister for a little while when she feels up to it. I also get to spend time with patients like my sister and other kids with sick siblings like me.

I'm so glad I get to be with my sister, my family, and all of these kids!

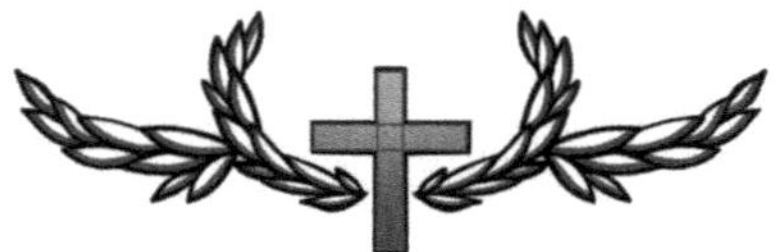

But then, things change again. Today my parents tell me Ari is worse, and I can't visit her for a while.

Tonight, all the parents and families at Target House gather in a big room to pray for all the sick children. There are people from many different countries, praying in different ways, different languages.

I have a warm feeling in my heart. I pray really hard, too.

I see that children from all over the world can get sick just like Ari did.

I see that no matter how different we might be, in here we are all the same!

My sister is moved to another place in the hospital called the ICU. Now I can only see her through the window, and I don't think she can see me at all.

Days piled up into a week and Ari seems to be okay one moment and really sick the next.

I can see how upset my family is.

I wish I could wake up. I wish this was a very bad dream!

She is so sick.

I am so scared.

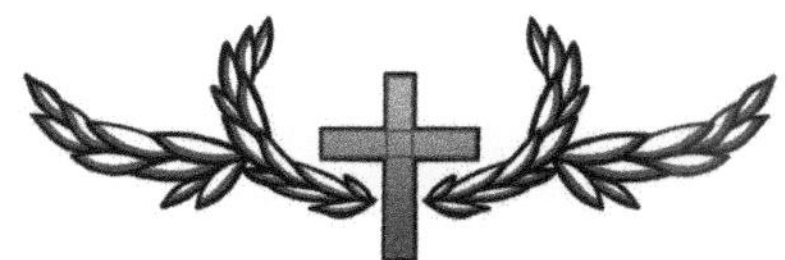

The next morning, I am playing on the playground. I see my dad coming to get me. We head up to Ari's room. I don't really want to go. Seeing her so sick makes me feel awful. I just want to play.

But before we get there, my dad stops and crouches down so his face is near mine. "Honey, I don't know how to say this," he whispers, "but your sister has died."

We reach her room and I see my big sister, but she just looks like she is sleeping. My mom is lying next to her holding her hand.

Many doctors and nurses are there with my family. Everybody is crying.

Why are they crying? She is sleeping, right?

I know my dad said she has died, but I don't understand what that means, not really. Does it mean she can never wake up?

Will I never see her again?

The machines and strings are no longer attached to her. She is free of them.

I cry too, but I don't want to stay in that room.

A nurse comes and asks if I would like to go to the art room to make something special for my sister. I go with her gladly.

I write messages to send to my sister in heaven. We place them inside of big balloons and then we go down back to the playground to release each of them into the sky!

I love you Ari!

Come back. Please!

What I am going to do without you?

I need you!

Is the threefold cord holding us together, even now?

Even if you are in heaven and I am here?

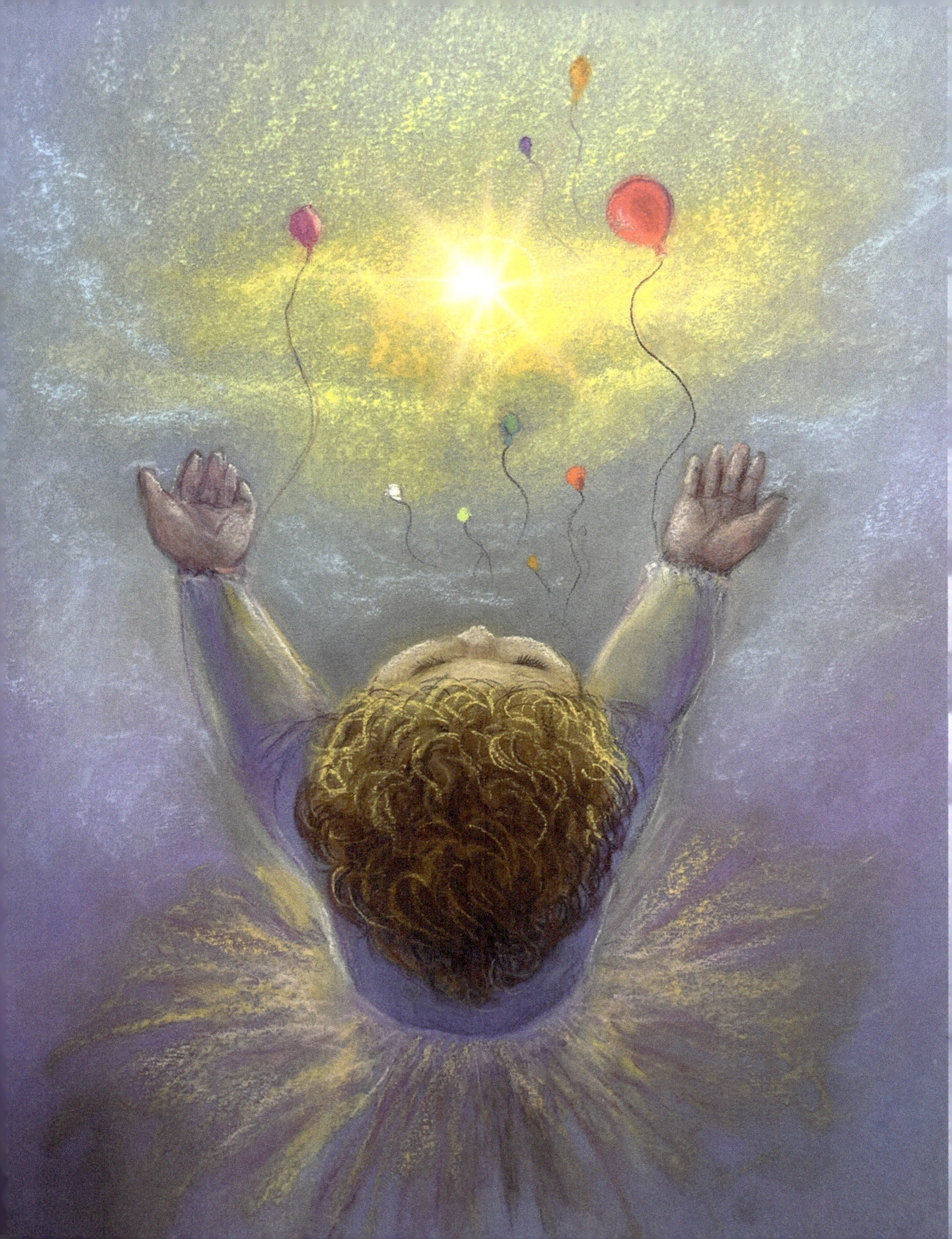

Part Two

The days that follow seem gray. It's like everything has lost its color.

I look outside the window and see the hospital far away. Right below my gaze is the playground where the other kids are playing. One of them sees me and calls me down. I don't feel like playing, but my dad holds my hand and takes me downstairs.

On the playground, my friend tells me how sorry she is that my sister has passed away. She says her brother is also very sick, and he might die too! We hug each other and cry.

My chest hurts. It must be because my heart is broken. I can't believe my sister is gone. She is truly gone!

The other kids stand and look at us, big-eyed, teary eyed.

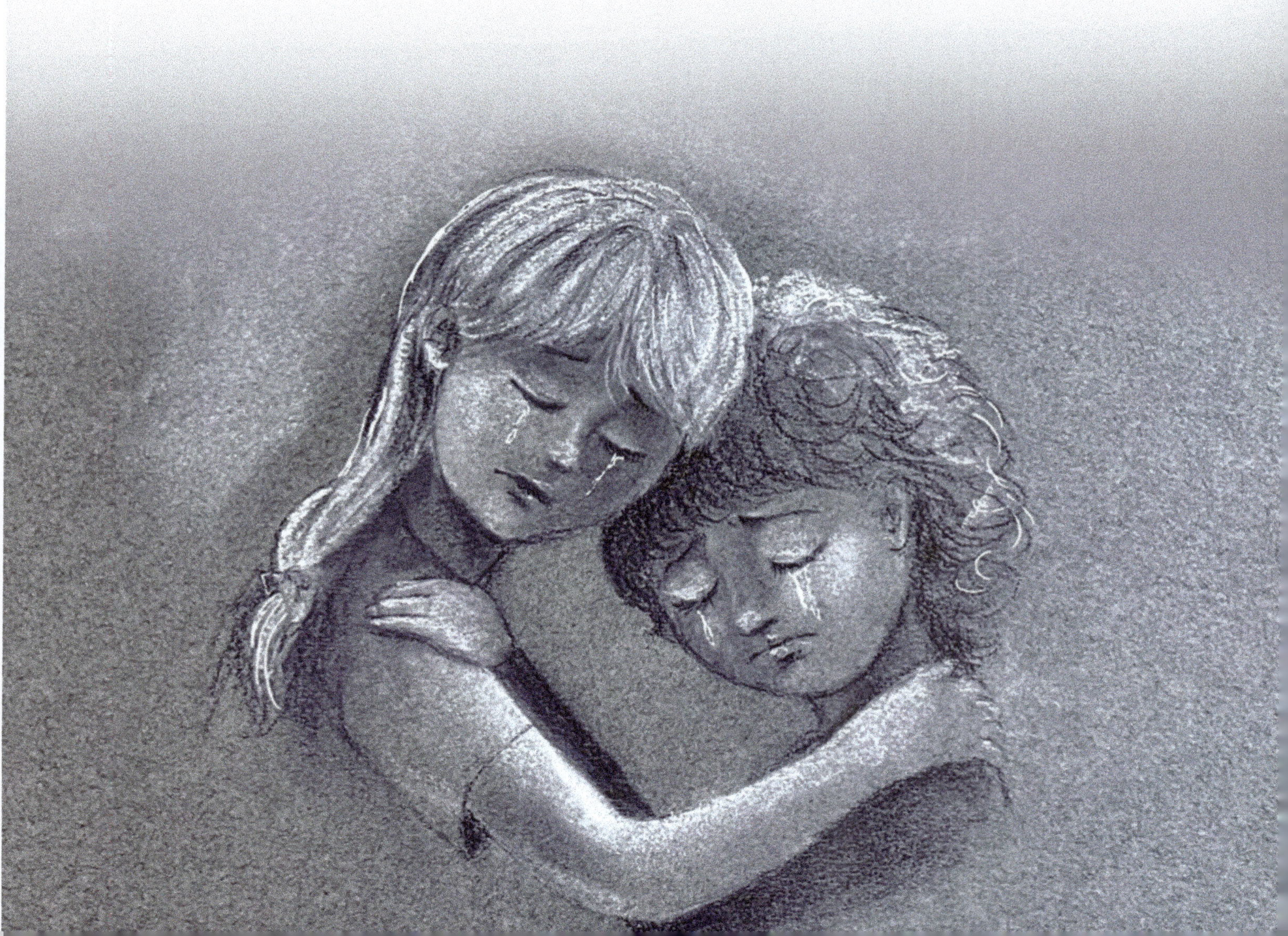

Later that night Mom is tucking me in bed.

"Mama, I miss my sister," I say. "Is she gone forever?"

"No, my love," she says. "When your sister died, an invisible part of her, the part that made her who she was, her unique self, went to heaven.

"The day she died on earth she was born into heaven. Her death was just the beginning of her life in heaven, where she is alive and well in the presence of God."

I feel better. Hopeful. But then a thought saddens me.

"Mom," I say, "I hate that she was so sick. Many times, I felt guilty because I wasn't sick like her. Because I'm still here and she isn't. I know she is in heaven, but why did she have to die?"

"My love, people die for different reasons. For her, it was her illness and it wasn't anyone's fault, not yours, not mine, not anyone else's. You must never feel guilty about it.

"I don't understand why your sister became ill, and I certainly don't understand why we ended up losing her. But sometimes we simply need to trust in God's sovereignty. Even though her life wasn't long, I believe with all of my heart that she did complete the purpose God had for her here on this earth.

"We must remember that she is no longer sick nor suffering because there is no sickness or suffering in heaven. In heaven there is only love, perfection, and joy greater than anything we can experience here on earth. And guess what? Someday we will see her again in heaven!

"Knowing that makes a difference, doesn't it, Love?"

I look at Mom with tears in my eyes, feeling very sad still.

Then Mommy hugs me gently and continues. "I know, my love, I know. It is good to know that she is well in heaven. But the truth is that we still miss her, and right now we hurt very deeply. We were prepared to love your sister, not to lose her. Being apart from her seems terrible, even unfair.

"The days ahead of us will be very difficult. We will feel pain, sadness, confusion, even anger, and that's OK. It is part of going through grief. We must feel all of our feelings so that our broken hearts can be mended and strengthened.

"Know that no matter how you feel, no matter how we feel, God's love for us will never change. And our love for you will never change, either. As hard as it may be at times, we need to listen to God's voice in the midst of our sorrow. He is all around us. I believe He will give us what we need. He will give us strength, peace, comfort – everything we need!"

But I am still worried.

"Mommy, what if I am mad at God for taking Ari to heaven? Will God love me still, even if I am angry at Him? Will He be with me and help me?"

"Yes! Nothing can separate us from His Love. Nothing. Not even our anger towards Him. His love endures forever, through everything. He created us and knows us better than we know ourselves. He knows it is difficult for us to make sense of Ari's death. He understands we get angry, and He forgives us and loves us anyway.

"Remember that you can talk to Him. Let Him know how you feel, even if it is ugly. He will listen and comfort you, and He will heal you with His never-ending love."

I tell my mom that I want to cry but I'm afraid that if I start, I won't be able to stop.

"My Beloved, don't hold your tears in," she says. "Our tears let our feelings flow out of our bodies. They cleanse us, they help us heal, so that one day we are able to find happiness again."

"But Mommy, I don't want to be happy if that means I'm going to forget my sister! I don't want to forget her!"

"Oh, Honey, no. Even though your sister is no longer here with us, we are connected still and we will never forget her. Never, ever! Remember the cord made of love and faith? Even now, the cord connects us to your sister – all the way to Heaven! Remember the cord is strong, it's unbreakable, unchangeable, and through it our love lives on forever.

"Your sister has not disappeared. She still exists. She lives in our hearts, in our memories, in the love we shared for one another, and in the lessons she taught us.

"My Love, I believe your sister is with us in many ways. Her voice will come to us when the breeze of a windy day whispers into our ear. We will feel her embrace in the warmth of a ray of sunlight. She will kiss our cheeks in the rain that falls unexpectedly. When sadness comes, listen and feel for her."

That night I have a dream I am playing with my sister at the beach, just like we did before she got sick.

It is a good dream!

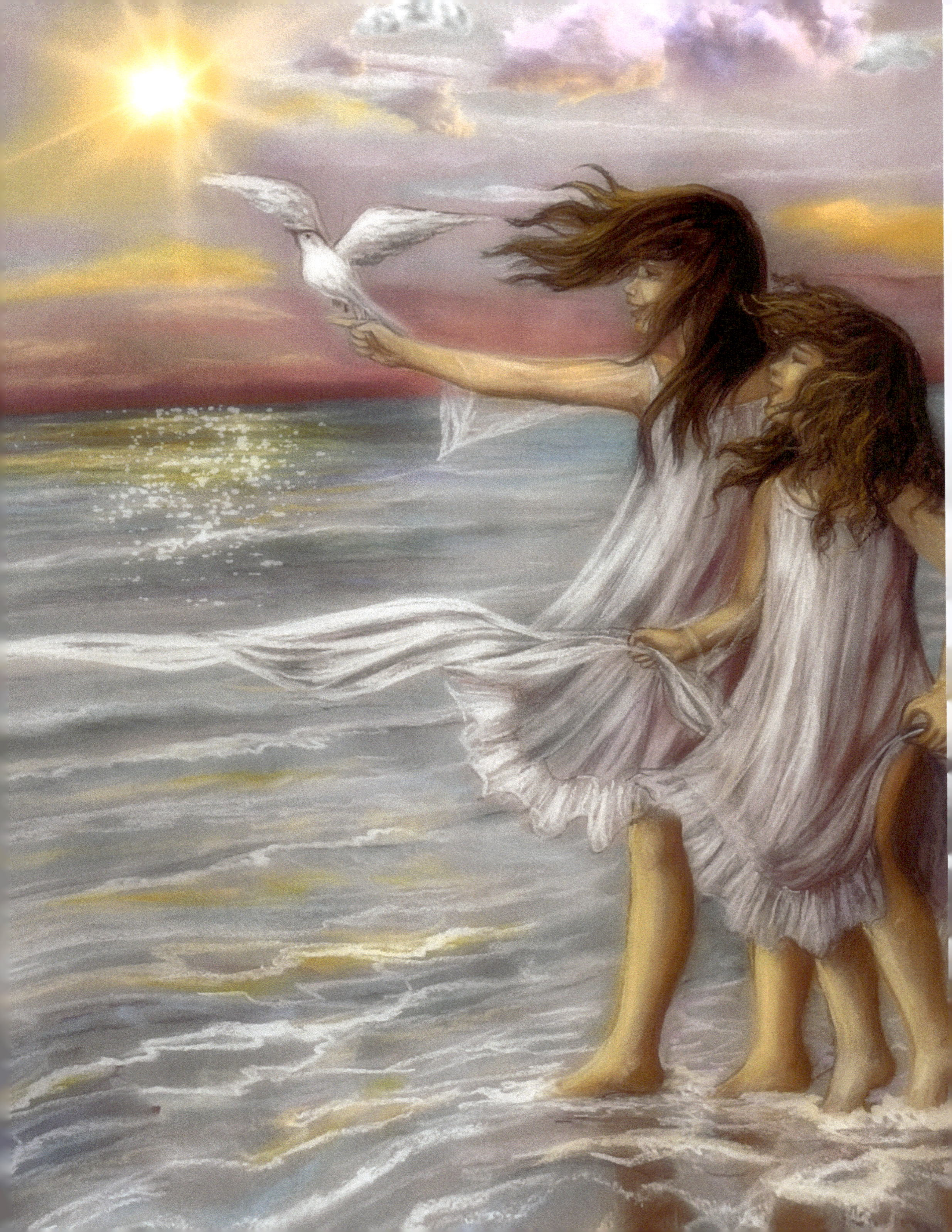

The next day we drive back home. It is snowing.

I turn around to tell Ari we should play in the snow when we get home. But her seat is empty, and I remember. She isn't here anymore!

I feel an immense gaping hole in my heart and in my life. Sadness and confusion take hold of me again.

I will make a snow angel for her when I get home. Maybe she will send me a hug from heaven when she sees it.

We arrive home late at night.

It is so dark that we need a flashlight for Mommy to find her key and open the door. When she does, a bird flies right into the house! It sits on top of a silk flower arrangement that my sister and I made together. It watches us for a moment and then flies a few circles around us. My heart is racing as it flies back out into the cold, wintry night.

I don't understand what has happened, but it feels very good.

Suddenly we remember Ari's promise – that she would come home with us, no matter what. Mom says that she believes this is a sign from God, for He knows we miss my sister very much.

I believe that, too! I believe Ari kept her promise!

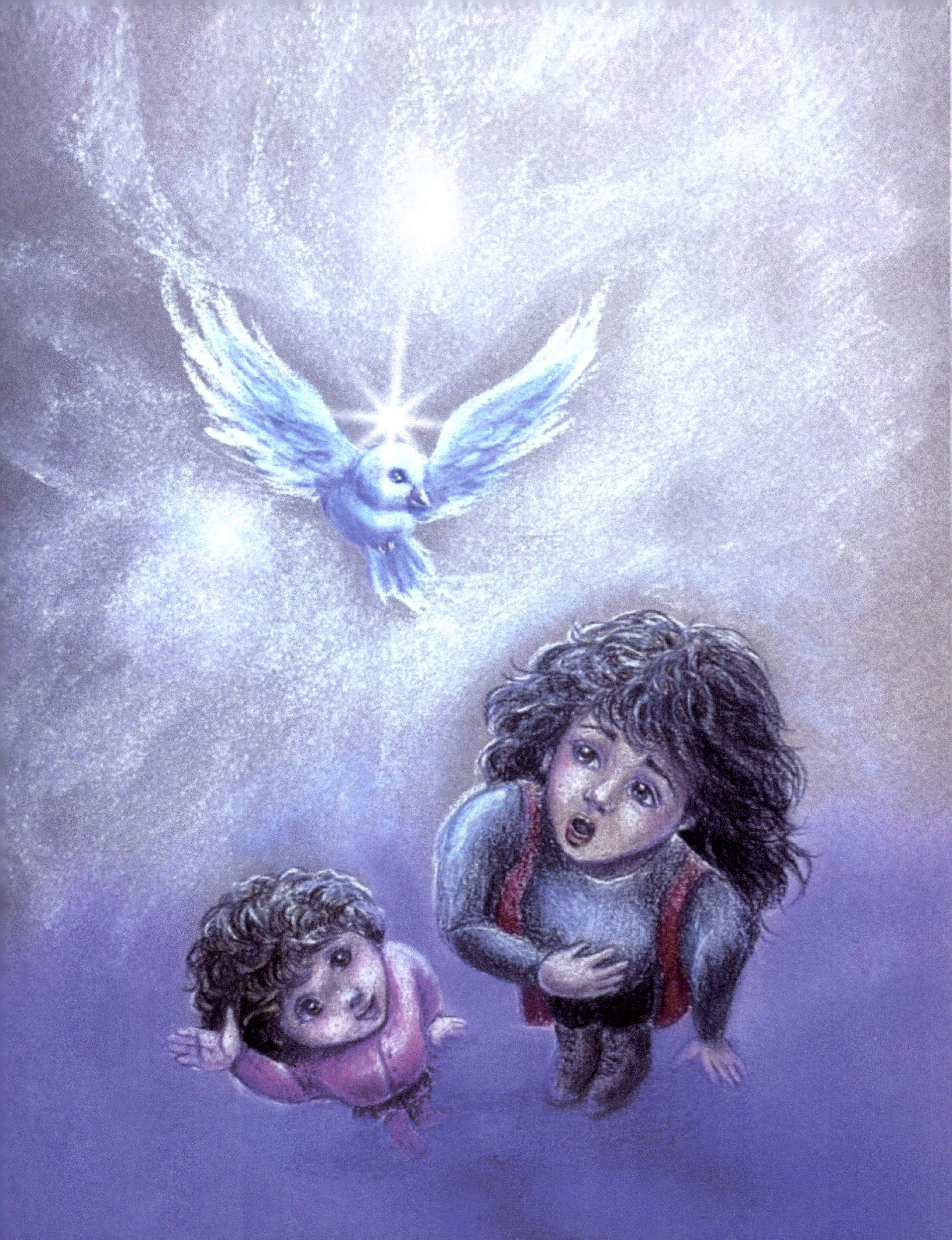

A few days go by and I still find it so hard to believe that my sister is gone.

I think my parents understand how strange this is for me. They are trying to be extra loving, but, frankly, I don't know what to do with all their attention.

Sometimes I just want to be left alone. But then my loneliness feels so enormous, it's overwhelming.

At times, I feel very angry. But I'm not sure why.

There are moments I don't feel anything at all. And there are moments my pain feels unbearable.

To help me cope, my parents take me to see a therapist. She is teaching me about grief and how to heal so I can feel well again.

I make drawings of my sister in heaven. It makes me hurt a little less to imagine her there. I think it helps my parents, too. Their eyes sparkle with tears, but I think they are happy tears!

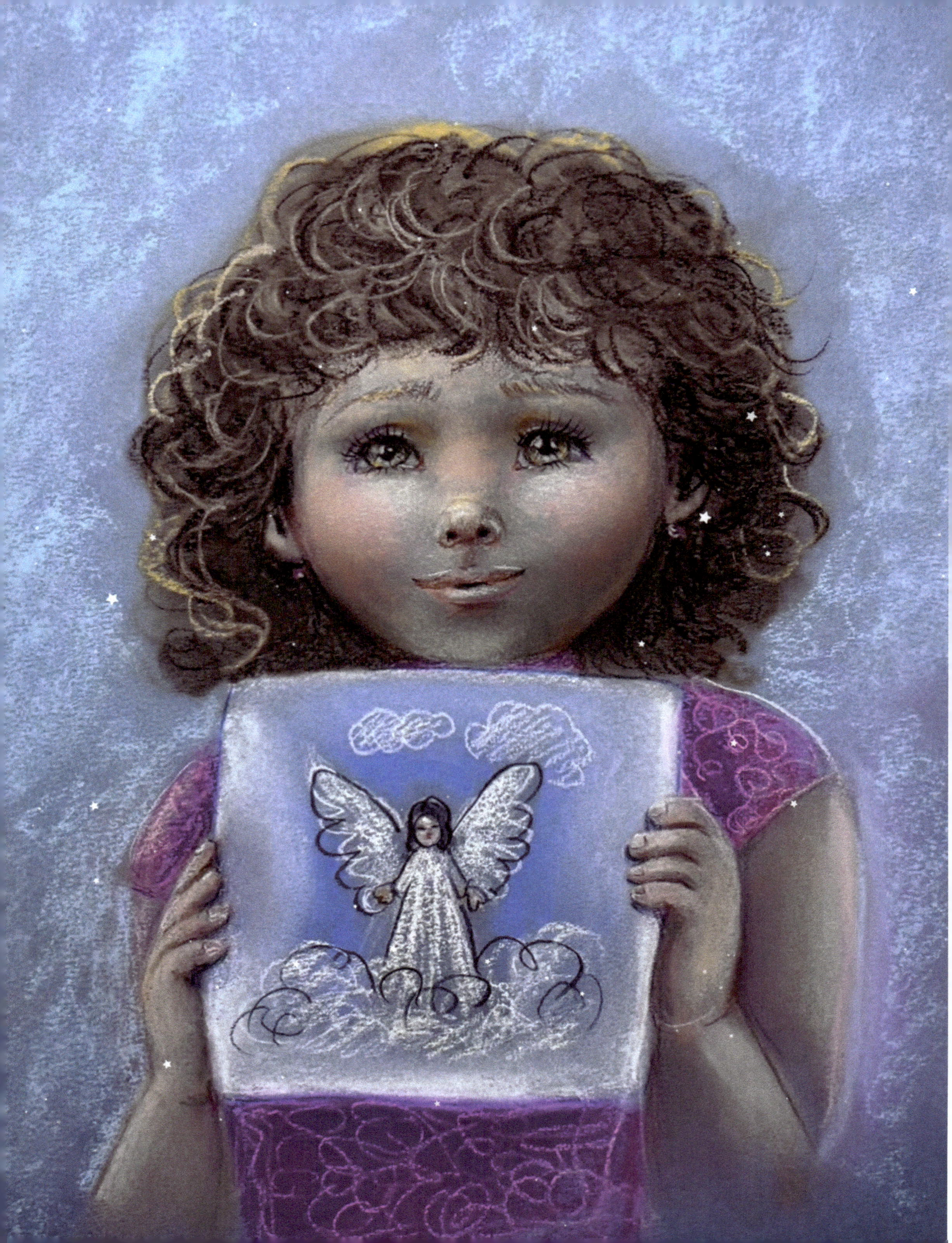

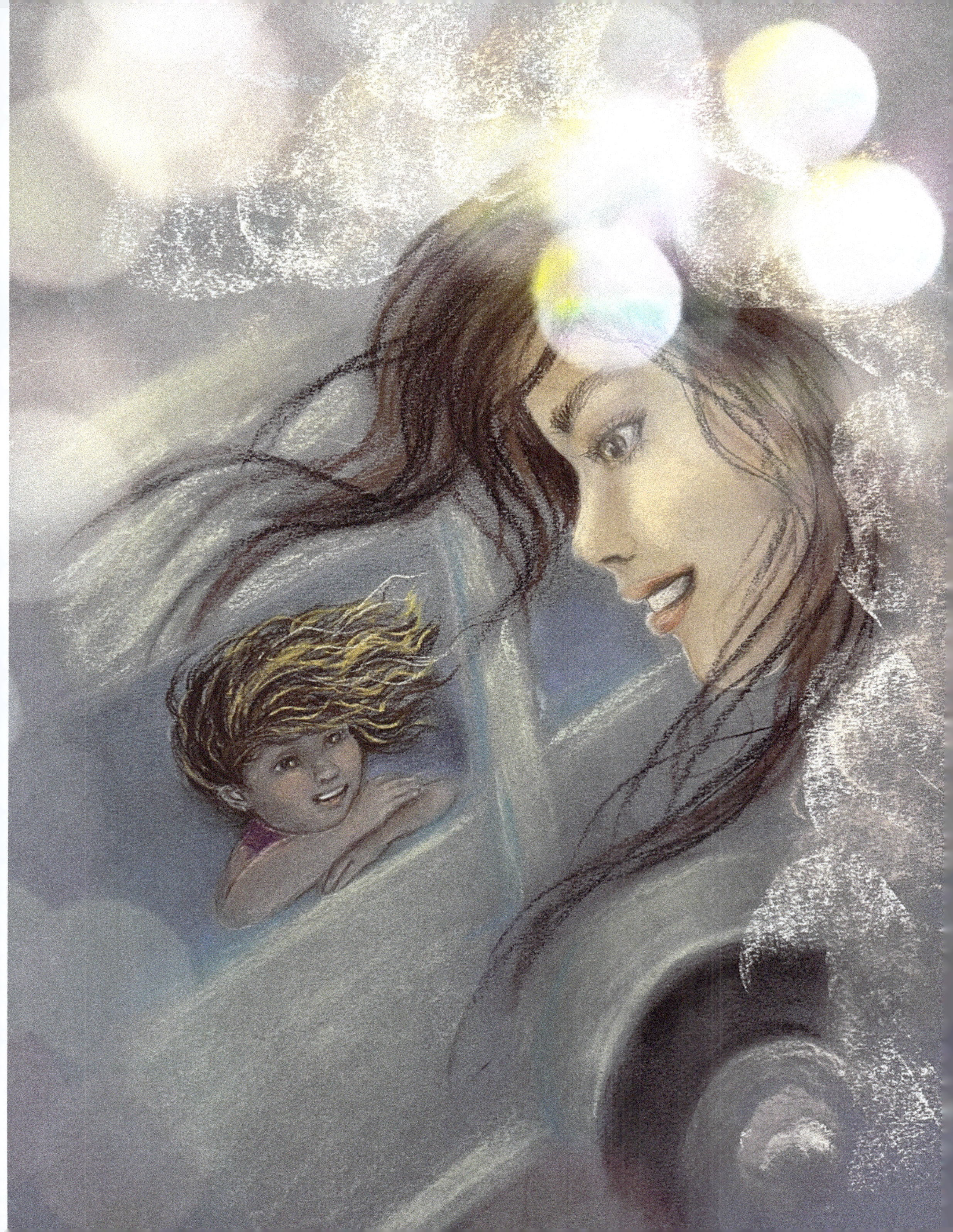

A ray of sunshine comes through the window this morning and softly touches my face. It feels like my sister waking me up!

"Wake up, wake up, Rose!" she used to say, and she would not leave me be until I did. So, I open my eyes and get up with a feeling that today is going to be a good day.

Dad walks into the bedroom and is surprised to find me wide awake.

"Honey Bunny, let's have breakfast and get ready quickly. We have a very special surprise for you!"

It is a bright day. The sky is filled with puffy clouds. I open the car window and the wind rushes in to play with my hair, making it all messy. I turn around to laugh with Ari, and once again, I feel that hole in my chest when I realize she's not there. But then I imagine her laughter in the sound of the wind, and I beam a big smile at her. I know she smiles back at me all the way from heaven!

We arrive at the house of one of my mom's friends from work.

"Come on in, Rose," she says. "We have a special gift for you."

The nice lady goes into another room and comes back holding something wrapped up in a pink baby blanket. She asks me to come closer to see my surprise. When I unwrap the blanket, I can't believe my eyes!

It is a precious puppy dog!

When I hold it, it starts licking my face and I feel this tickling sensation all the way down to my tummy. I feel so happy! I start laughing and laughing, and the tiny little puppy just keeps licking and tickling my face.

"Rosie" says the nice lady. "I want you to think of the puppy as a gift from your sister Ari. She will be a special companion for you, to remind you that is OK to feel joy again – for when you are happy, your sister is celebrating your gladness all the way from heaven!"

I name my puppy Princess. I love her so!

I realize that I can feel happy, and when I do, I am not forgetting my sister, but honoring her memory.

Somehow, I know in my heart I can share my happiness with her even now!

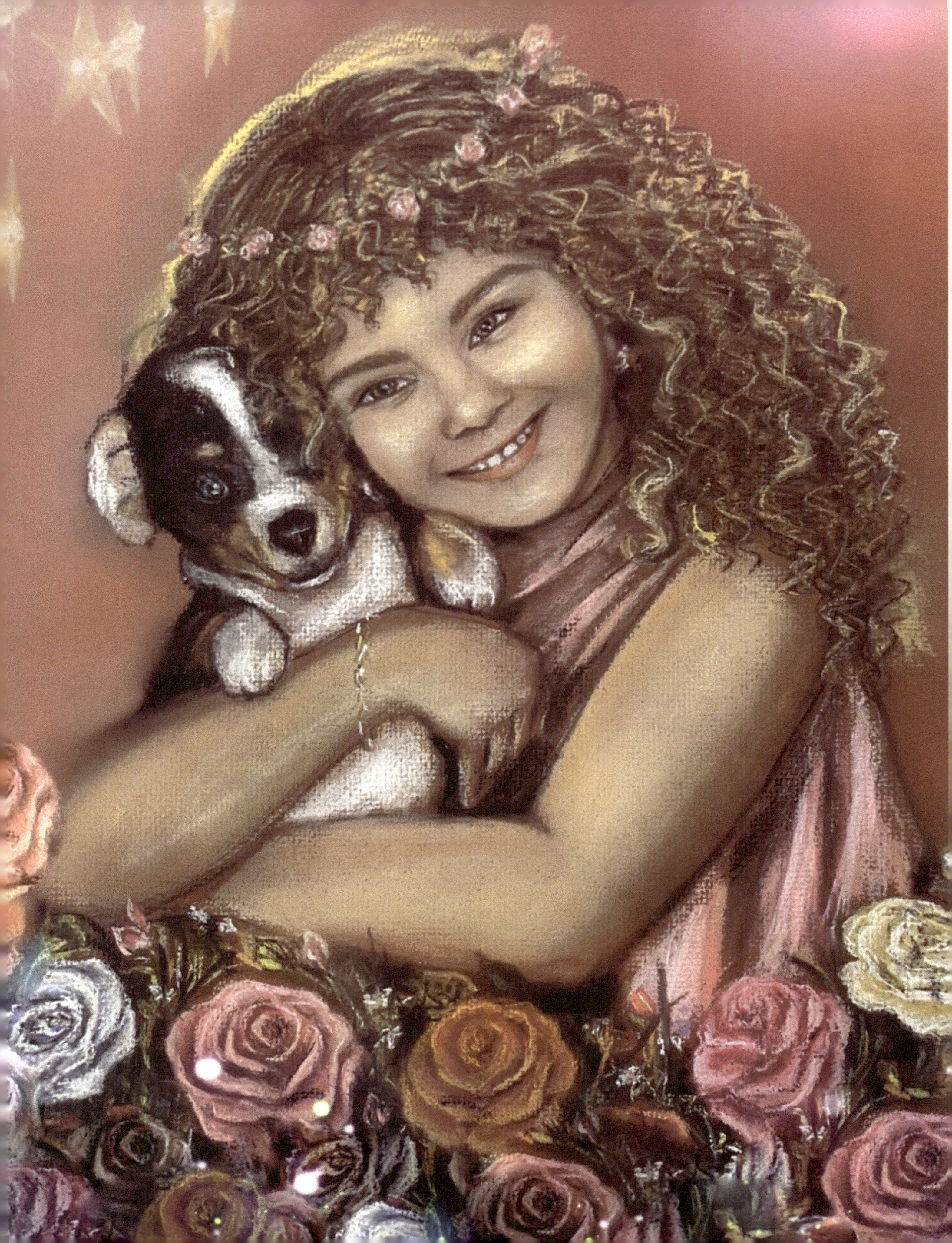

Days turn into weeks, weeks into months and months into years.

At times, I find myself grieving still. Grieving, not only for the things I lost when my sister died, but also for the things I continue to lose.

We are invited to what would have been Ari's high school graduation to talk to all the kids. I can almost see Ari sitting right there, listening, feeling very proud, shining with a huge grin on her beautiful face!

Sometimes I wonder how life would be if she hadn't died.

I think I will always miss my sister. But even in my sadness, even in my darkest moments, I am reminded that I have a certainty that only God can give me. The certainty that my sister is well and I will see her again.

The certainty that gives me hope.

The hope that replaces my feelings of shock with calm.

The hope that replaces my devastation with peace.

The hope that replaces my denial with acceptance.

The hope that replaces my anger with glee.

The hope that replaces my fear and panic with faith.

The hope that replaces my heartache with comfort.

The hope that replaces my guilt with forgiveness.

The hope that replaces my depression with joy and my loneliness with companionship.

The hope that embraces me and reminds me that our love will never, ever die!

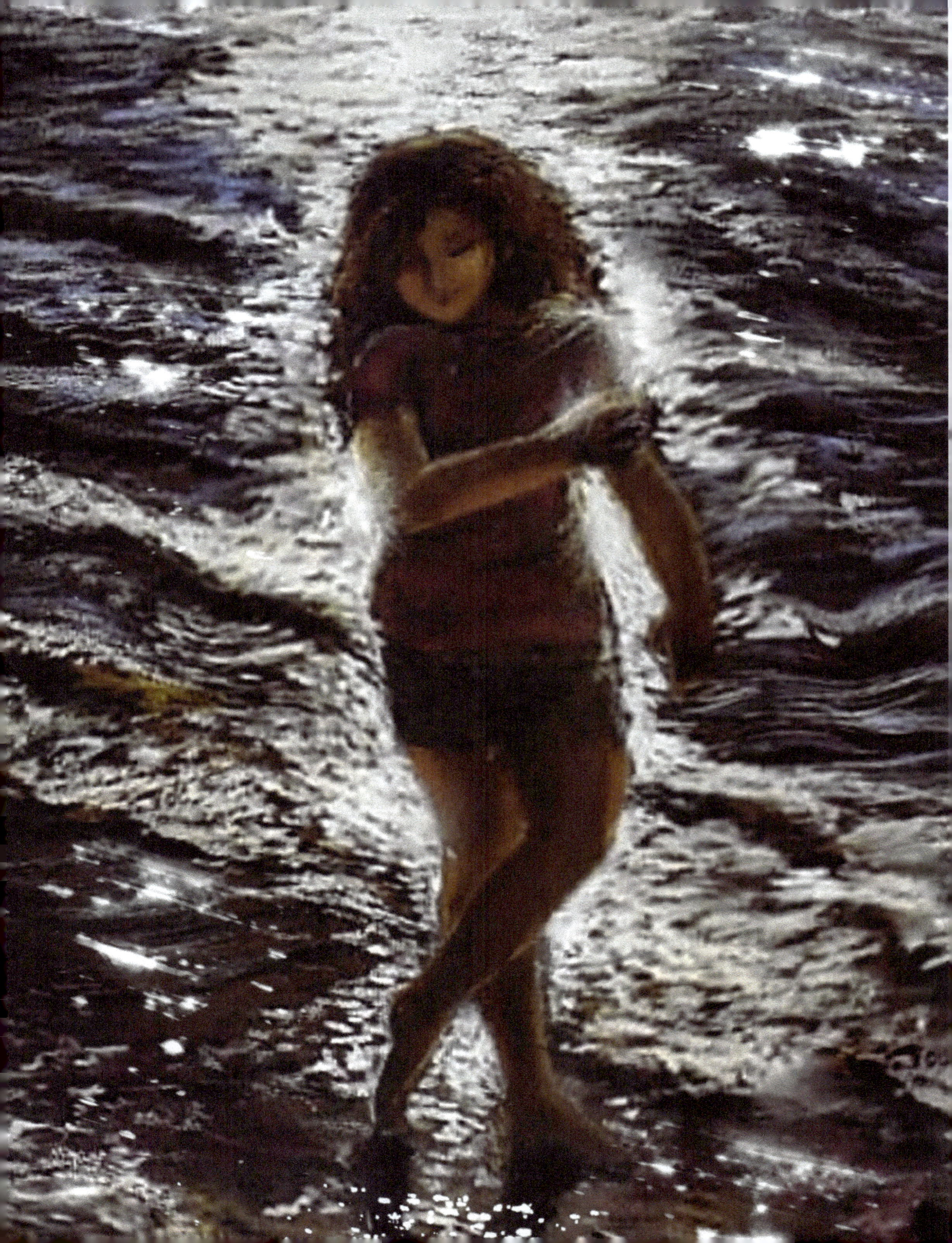

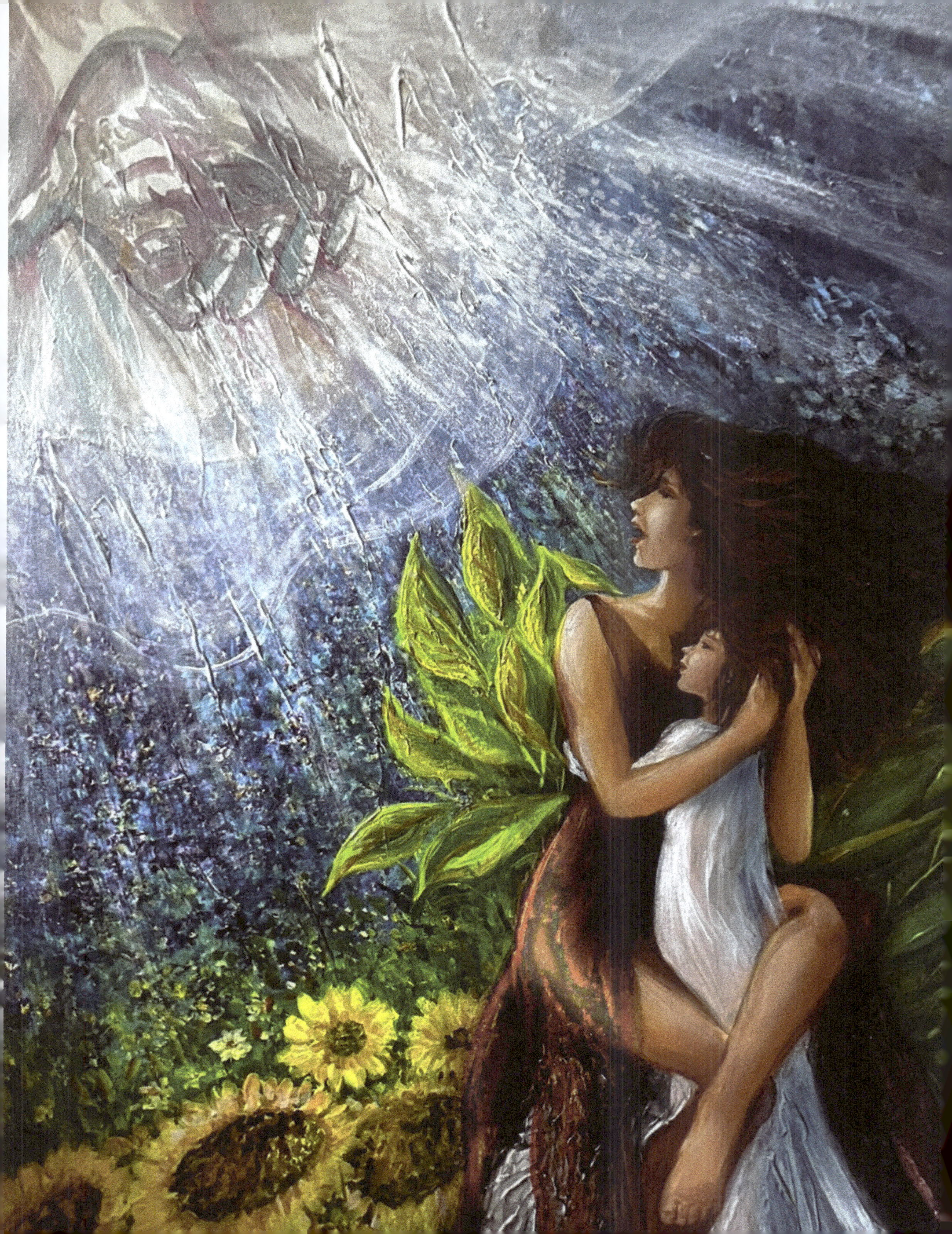

The Mother's Journey

A Goodbye

On March 1st, 2004, I gave the last hug to my daughter Ariadna. I climbed into her bed and embraced her.

She could not respond for she was in a coma.

Like telling her a secret, I whispered into her ear: "Go on with the Lord, My Love. Your mom will be fine; we will be fine!"

I have given her permission to surrender her body, so weary and shattered by the terrible disease and the ruthless chemotherapy treatment.

Seconds later, she gave way to her very last breath. A few heartbeats afterwards saw her emptying the earthy vessel that could no longer hold her prisoner.

And then, unexplainably, I felt her spirit elevate and soar…

Free at last, bound for the eternal!

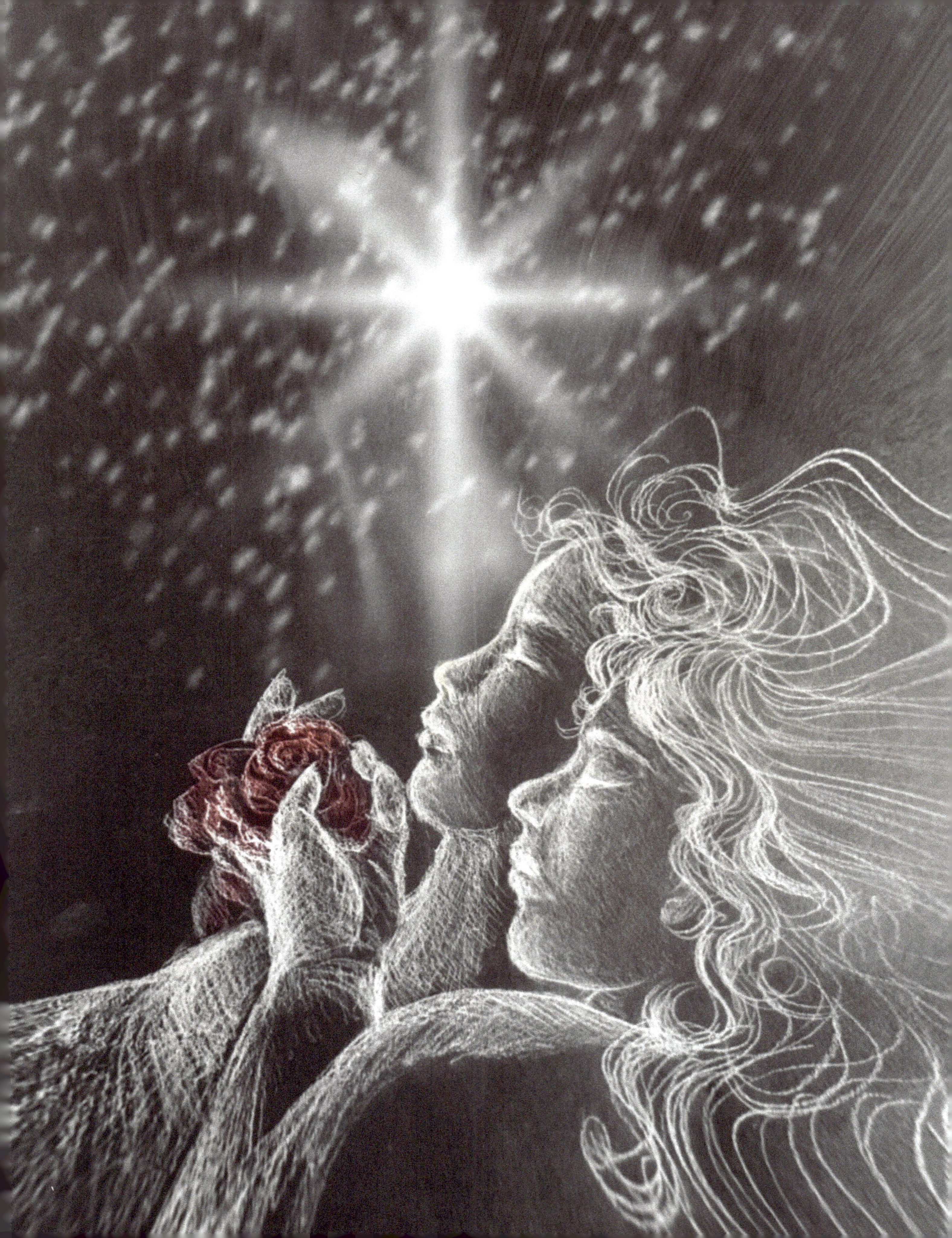

Our Forever

Broken heart and yet I knew
the marvelous, the wondrous, was revealed to you
Glorious beyond imagination
Your new life began without hesitation

The eternal joy forever unveiled
Your spirit soared like a swallow-tail

Freedom and love
Lightness, all heaviness gone!
Don't look behind my sweet darling
Don't look behind
You left behind pain,
Illness and suffering
Our love followed you as an eternal offering

Shattered in pain and desperation
We cried out for help with tears of desolation
You and I in one accord
Crying out to the One Above

I finally understood there was no mending
Your earthly journey was soon to be ending

You were barely holding on to life...

I wanted you here,
But my love for you spoke louder
Love kept us hoping for
Love kept us holding on
And now Love was begging for a goodbye

I whispered into your ear:
"Go on to be with the Lord, My Dear"
And in one exhale your journey to eternity began
Set free and weightless
Healed and ageless
Limitless and restored
All sickness was gone

Don't look behind, My Sweet Darling
Don't look behind
You left behind pain,
Illness and suffering
Our love followed you as an eternal offering

Longing for you everyday
Bittersweet the hope and the sorrow
Hand-in-hand dancing through many tomorrows

Sometimes I find you in the sky
And then I realize
You are all around me
Peering through the clouds
Whispering in the wind
As in the gentle breeze caressing my skin

Our love keeps us together
This love is strong for it is made of forever

True love knows no barriers
Neither time, nor distance
Nor life or even death
can affect its existence!

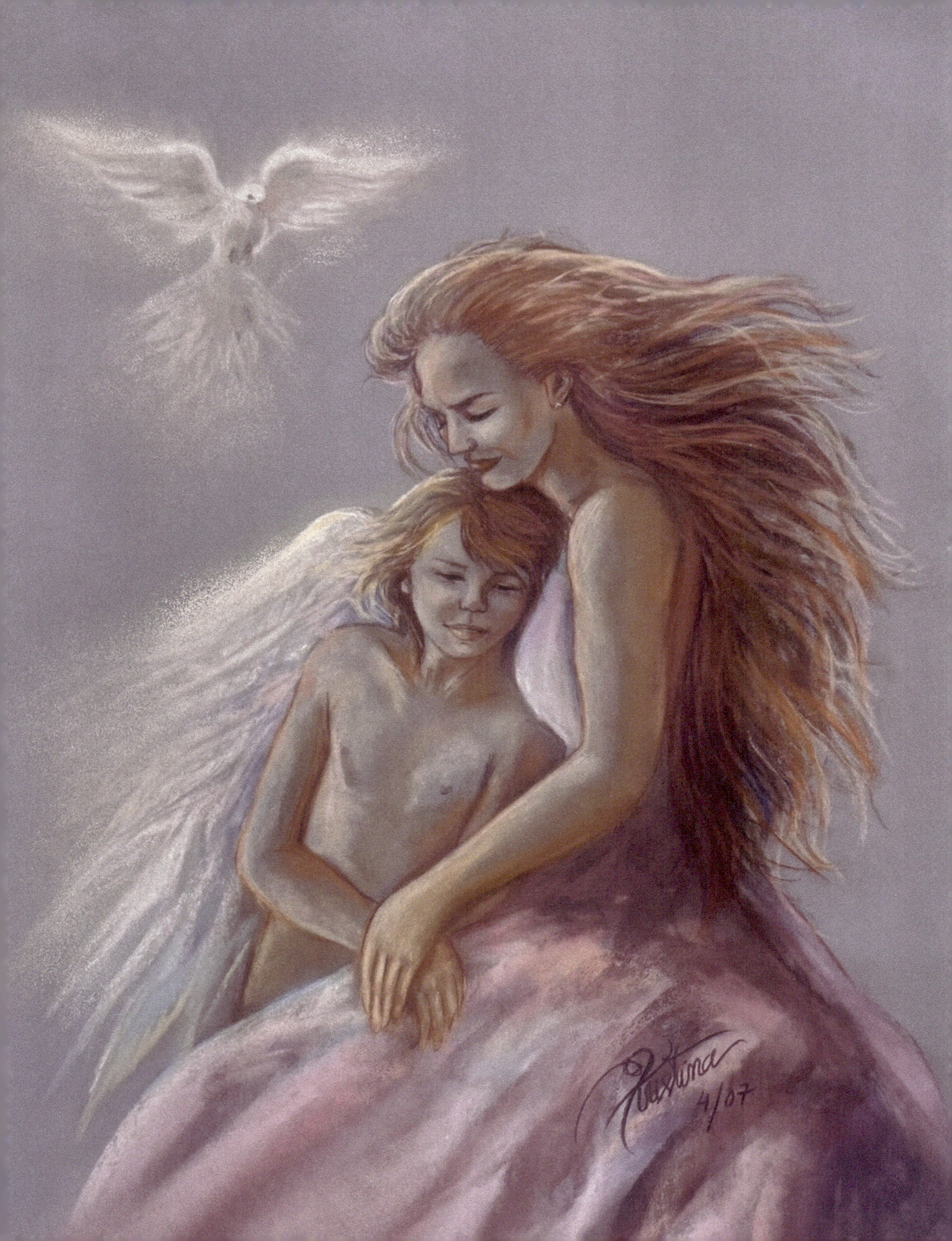

The Winged Visitation

The last time we flew to St. Jude Hospital after we were told of her relapse, Ariadna made me a promise. She said: "Mami, it's okay, I promise I will come back home with you!"

Her words gave me the strength I needed to face the battle for her life that was waiting ahead.

Almost three months later we were coming home without her.

My child had passed away!!!

In my utter brokenness I couldn't stop thinking of her words and the cruel reality that followed me home.

She was gone, and I was on my way home without her!

I wanted it to stop, to linger, to stay in that moment she made her promise. I wanted to wake up from the nightmare that stole her life away.

Anything that would keep me from having to face the inevitable. I did not want to enter our home without her.

We arrived at nine p.m. on a wintry night so dark, the stars refused to shine.

Dreadfully, I stepped into the house, and from the pitch-black frigid sky, a bird flew inside our home with me. It glided above my head a few times and gently landed on a flower arrangement Ariadna had helped us make.

It sat there for a few moments, watching me intently. My eyes connected with the little creature. In the depths of my heart a sensation like nothing I had experienced before began to take form: a Knowing, a Hope, a Peace.

As if transcending this reality, I felt with certainty that Ari had kept her word. She had come home with me as she promised.

A few seconds later the winged visitor flew off, out the door, and into the night.

It was after nine p.m. in the middle of a wintry night.

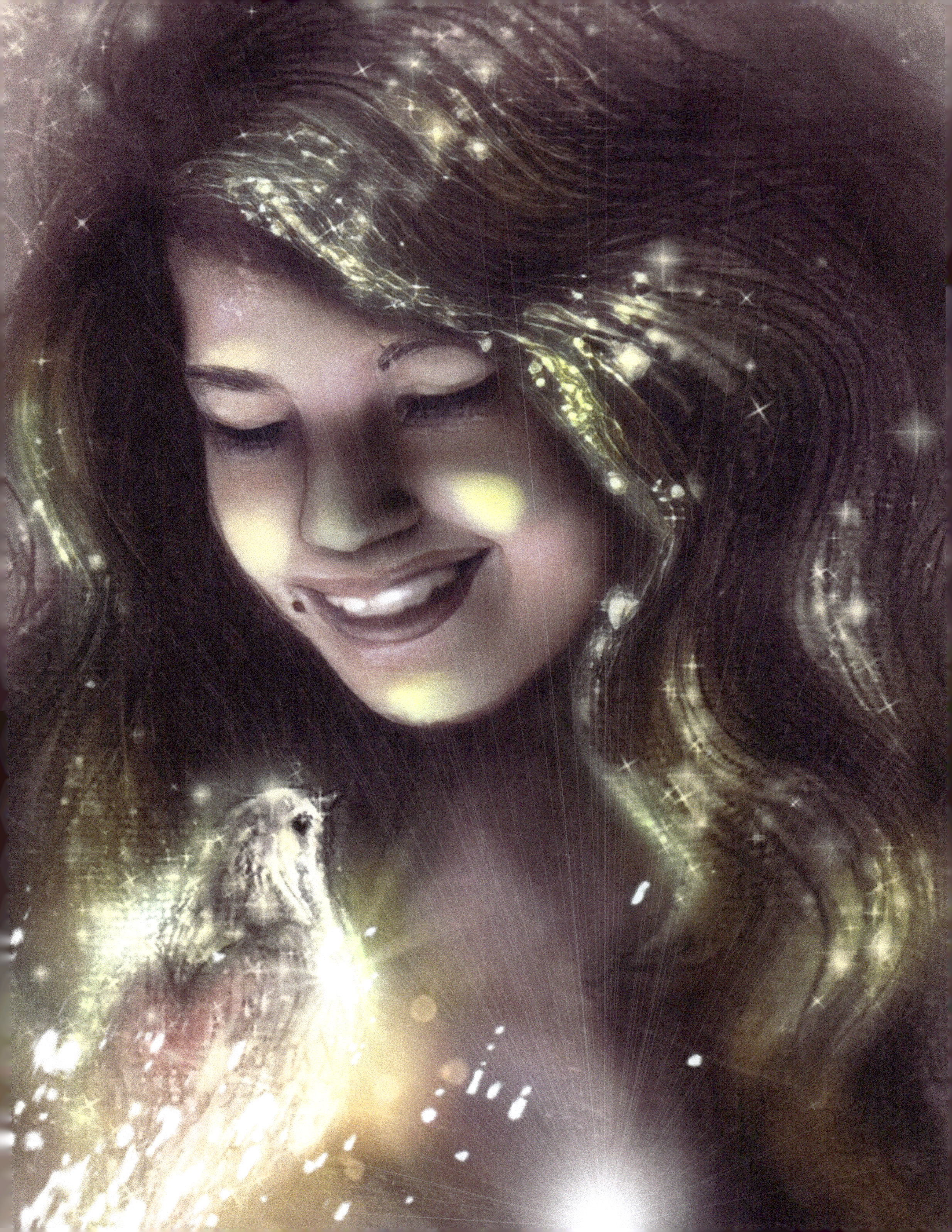

The Vision

A few days had gone by since I lost my child.

A blink of an eye and an eternity all at the same time.

My heart laid utterly broken, sunken in a darkness so deep, a parent should never know.

It was during one of those elongated nights of agony that I experienced something I shall never forget.

In an instant, there she stood – my beloved daughter, a few inches from me. My eyes examined her in disbelief and finally rested upon her glittering brown eyes. I knew then this wasn't a dream, because all of my senses were heightened. This was more real than reality.

As if I needed to offer proof to convince myself, I inched closer to her and in her presence I was drenched. There was no doubt in my heart. I was right there in front of my child.

But my beloved was older somehow, emanating a maturity, a wisdom and a light so immense it took me aback.

An adult version of herself, fully restored, healed and more beautiful than ever. The shock of recognition rattled me to the core.

My mind went wild and my body surrendered to the need to embrace her … and so I did.

I turned my face toward her neck and drank in her essence deeper still.

She stretched her hands gently reaching down to the sides of my shoulders. Feeling her touch, I pulled back a little to see her face again. She had something to say; I sensed it.

I stepped back to listen … all of my many questions on hold.

"Mom" - she uttered with a smile that irradiated the purest joy.

"Mami, I am better than I have ever been before. As short as my earthly life was, it fulfilled its intention. Now, I move further on to accomplishing the purpose for which I've been created.

I know you don't understand now … you will someday.

I know you miss me but know this: I am with you always.

I love you! *Te amo Mama*!"

She embraced me and a whisper of a kiss rested upon my right cheek.

And then, just as quickly as this vision began, it ended.

I was back in my bedroom, only this time, I was tightly holding with my entire being unto every image, every word, every scent, every sensation, the hope, the mystery of everything I had experienced.

I whispered: "I love You too" into the dark night knowing that somehow, she could hear.

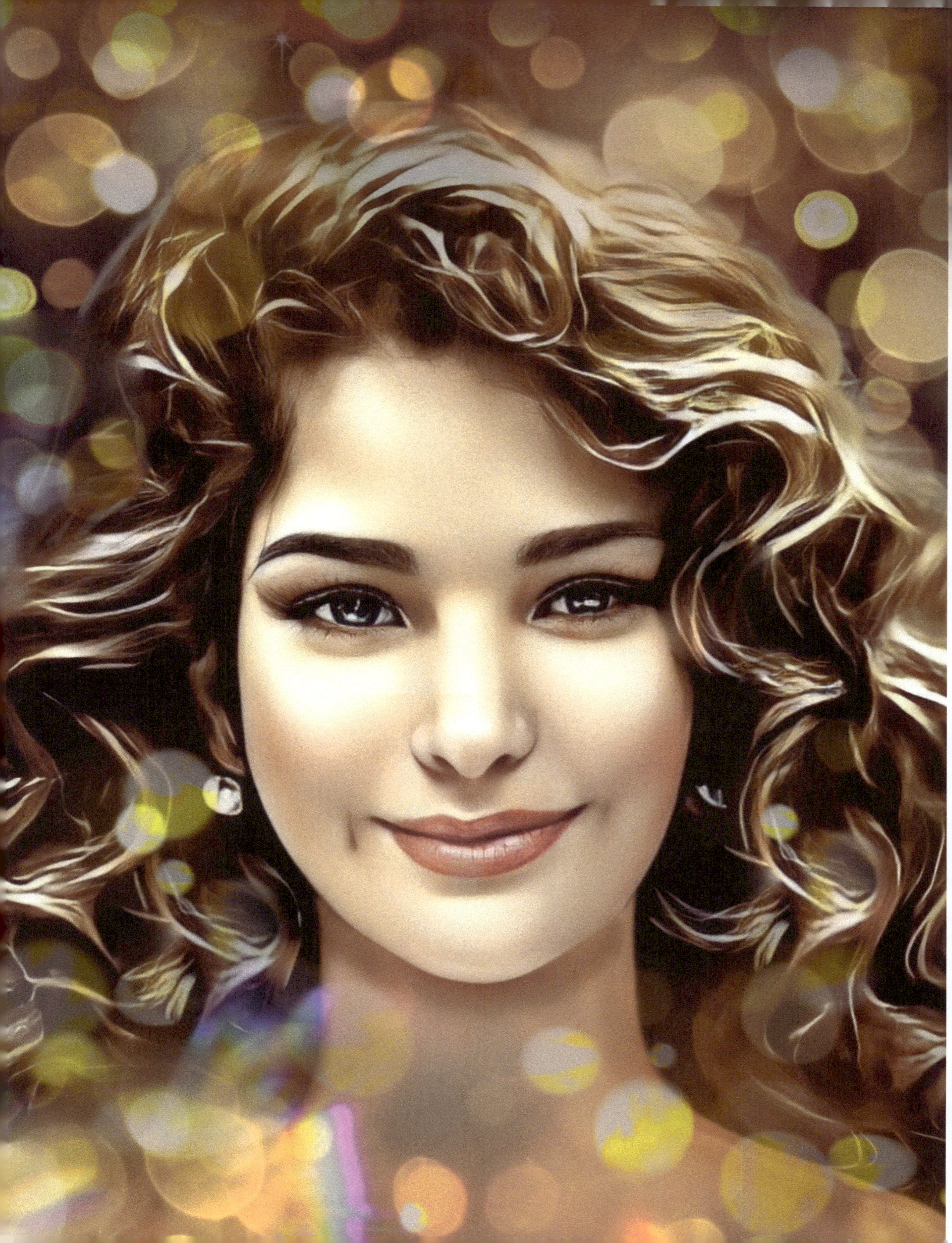

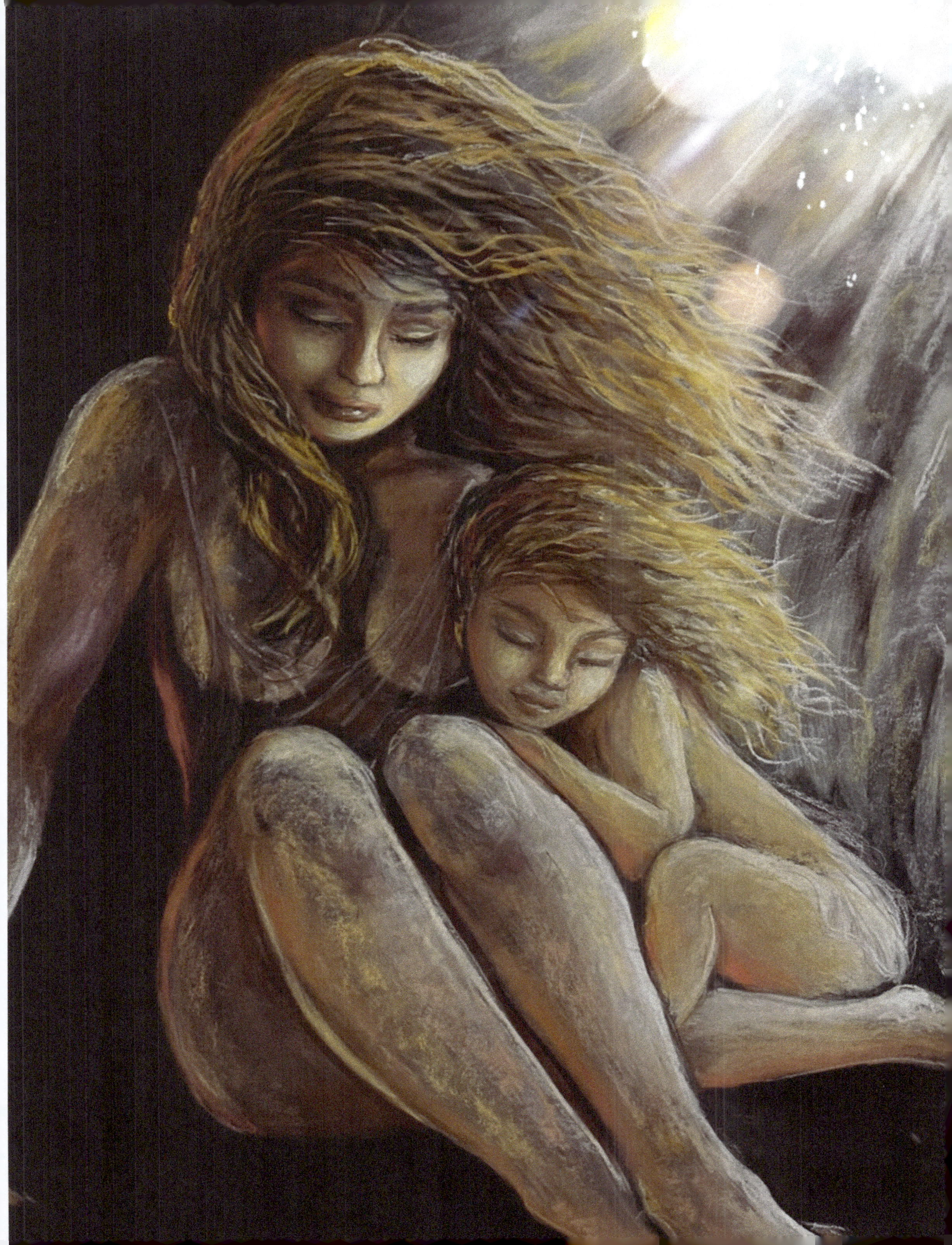

True love knows no barriers ...
neither time, nor distance,
or even death can affect its existence

Time passes,
but true love never passes

Life is but a moment
True love is endless
Distance cannot dim its light
Time cannot weaken its power

What is immortal lives on forever
The love that unites us will never be severed

The Miracle

The following occurred the first time my child relapsed, about four and a half years after the initial diagnosis.

My oldest child was healthy again.

We had finished the ruthless 3-year chemotherapy treatment protocol successfully.

One and a half years of being cancer-free and treatment-free had passed. Time found us expanding our wings, living life like there was no tomorrow.

We were involved in amazing things: choir, praise dance, swimming, soccer, art, cheerleading ... we were living life to the fullest!

Life was great. It seemed things were finally going our way!

Each day found us thanking God for the things most people take for granted.

We also knew pain intimately, for we knew what it was like to face death in the eye.

We had drunk from the bitter cup of childhood cancer, and we would never forget how it tasted.

God had been faithful. He had delivered my child, and with her, us too.

Nevertheless,

Out of the blue came a day of darkness. It knocked very hard on our door, broke it open and yanked us back into the nightmare!

We had to learn the terrible meaning of the word "relapse."

We were faced with the news Ari's cancer had returned. Our world was shattered.

I was submerged in a deep state of shock, despair, bitterness, anger, depression, denial, panic and a myriad of other sorrowful emotions!

The first time we battled cancer we did not know the nightmare that it would entail. But this time we knew, and this knowledge had wrecked us.

I *Could Not* understand what was happening.

I kept calling, but God wouldn't answer.

He seemed gone!

Days encountered me crying with tears tinged with anger and disbelief. I kept asking Him why had He turned his face from us?

Why had He abandoned us?

On the ninth day of this nightmare, I was too exhausted, too tired to argue or to ask why anymore.

That evening – I SURRENDERED.

I fell down on my knees and said: "Lord, please help me. I am listening."

Then suddenly a voice on the television became prevalent. I did not know the TV was on to begin with, and to this day, I still do not know who the dark-haired preacher was.

I knew God was going to speak to me somehow.

The man's message took me to Genesis' first chapter. After he read the scripture, he dived deeper into it.

While I don't recall everything that was said, the following stayed with me:

".... there was complete chaos, but God did not stop to contemplate it or dwell on it. Instead, He opened His mouth and uttered commands into the pandemonium. His Word accomplished the purpose for which it was sent: the light was separated from darkness, the land from the water. The disorder was replaced by God's order."

When the message ended, I walked towards my child's hospital bed. I felt compelled to impose my hands over her weary body.

Unexplainably, I sensed heat radiating outwards from both of my palms.

I remember opening my mouth, a prayer being spoken.

Then, as unfamiliar words flowed forth from my lips, I saw a vision:

Pitch black at first but gradually a light began to appear. The growing light traveled through unfathomable dark tunnels. I don't recall seeing such intense darkness ever before, but, as the light approached it, the darkness dissolved.

In each and every area the light flooded; darkness was overcome.

It felt like a very long journey. This comet-like beam of light did not stop until it had eradicated all obscurity. I knew, somehow, I was witnessing the cleansing of cancer cells from my child's body.

At some point it all ended. My vision and my prayer stopped also.

I was overtaken by a sense of warmth and peace.

My beloved 10-year-old girl was peacefully sound asleep for the first time in many days. Exhausted, I lay in the couch next to her bed, and within seconds I fell into a deep slumber. It was the first night we both slept soundly.

Around six a.m., a nurse woke me up. With my eyes half way open I answered her, and with a beaming smile, she said:

"Kristina! We ran the matinal tests and Ari's blood is clean! There are no cancer cells in her blood stream! We believe she may have entered remission!"

Oh my God! I knew how the remission came about; science was offering confirmation of the healing vision shown to me a few hours earlier.

A year of ups and downs followed. The new treatment protocol made the first look like a child's game. Each day came with a new challenge. Juggling extremes, fighting to focus on the good while facing the ongoing suffering of my child. We walked this roller coaster of a life dressed in hope and in faith.

But then,

To my dismay, two years later the cancer came back to stay.

I couldn't comprehend the reason why God revealed His power, bestowing healing of miraculous proportions, to later allow my child to succumb to the returning illness.

Some folks had their theories. They had to do with lack of Faith on our part.

It's easy to judge others when not walking in their shoes.

At first, I allowed those statements to become a tool for self-flogging and doubt. A tool to torture myself with the "what if I had somehow caused my daughter's illness to return and kill her."

But no, it wasn't because we did not have enough Faith. God taught us about Faith. He showed us His power in action!

What if Faith was the very key that granted us six extra years with our child after the initial diagnosis?

Sometimes we don't get what we want.

Sometimes the answer to our prayers is a different kind of Yes.

I believe she was healed. She was not granted a temporary healing on this earth.

Instead, God healed her for eternity!

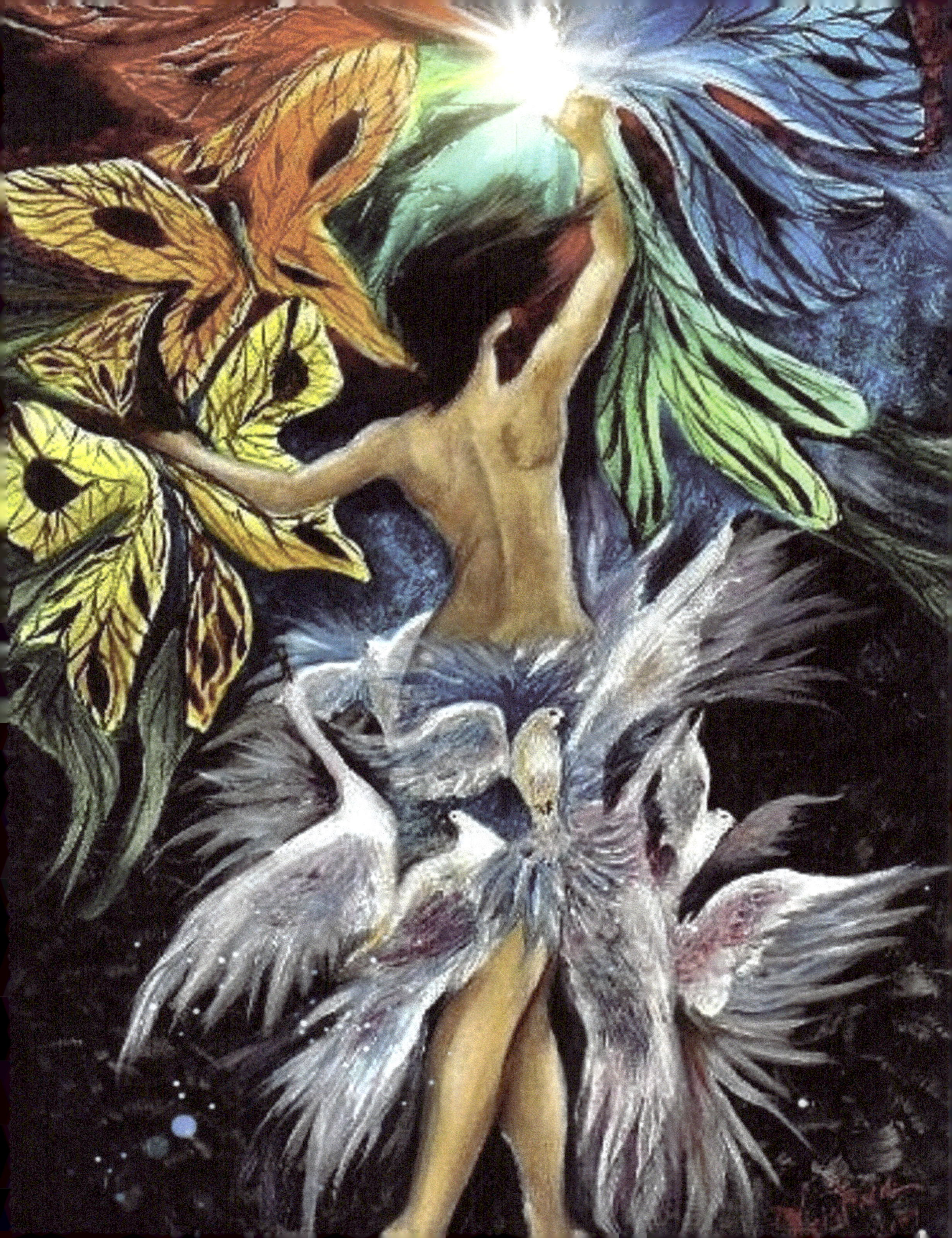

Another Anniversary

March 1st marks the anniversary of a day I wish I didn't have to remember.

A leap year saw my oldest daughter take her last breath. Her precious 12-year-old body became an empty vessel.

How do you make sense of such a loss? Parents are not supposed to bury their child after all! Right?

In my heart I was convinced - SHE WOULD MAKE IT!

I thought that if I did and believe the "right things" my child would be spared.

It was a simple enough recipe in theory that became more and more complex in reality. Keeping the Faith when things are going your way is very easy. But keeping the same Faith when things fall apart is not.

Amazingly at the end, it was Faith that sustained me during those years of contrasted dark and light. I cannot take credit for it. Faith was my only route. There was no other choice for me.

I worked very hard to believe, to have the faith and the strength to battle the war of our lifetime. The war for the life of my child, which ultimately would have the outcome I wanted. The outcome according to my will, not necessarily the Lord's.

But then, why would God allow that a child so beloved be taken from her mother's arms? From her family?

I may or may never know the answer.

Years later, I arrived at a conclusion. And as time passes, this conclusion has evolved into my conviction:

I am convinced that someday the response will no longer matter.

Someday, I know I will be with her.

The blink of an eye that this life was would have passed away, and with it, its queries and tribulations. A new life in eternity with my beloved will be unfolding.

No, I am not saying that her loss has been forgotten. It is impossible to forget your child.

Years later, it still hurts. I miss her so.

Society tends to forget that when you lose an important person in your life, it is not just a one-time-loss.

It has a ripple effect in your life. It becomes a series of losses: the birthdays, the graduations, the holidays, the unfulfilled dreams.

All of those milestones in life that we took for granted now come and go unfulfilled.

It is like a slap in the face or a cold bucket of water that falls on your head when you least expect it.

Years later finds me healing still.

I do not let anyone tell me how and for how long I am supposed to grieve.

We are all different and each individual relationship is unique.

I do not concern myself with people's judgments any longer. They are not me and have never, and will never, walk in my shoes.

I will treasure the time I was given with Ariadna for the rest of my life here on earth.

Together we lived some of the most beautiful years of our lives.

The darkness we experienced taught us to appreciate life. It taught us to value the things we take for granted – like being able to take your children for a swim and get soaked with joy as they squeal and giggle!

For the rest of my life, I will love my child and will not be ashamed to recognize my brokenness and my hope in the Lord's promise that HE IS STILL IN CONTROL, even in the midst of this painful loss.

He is my strength when I am weak.

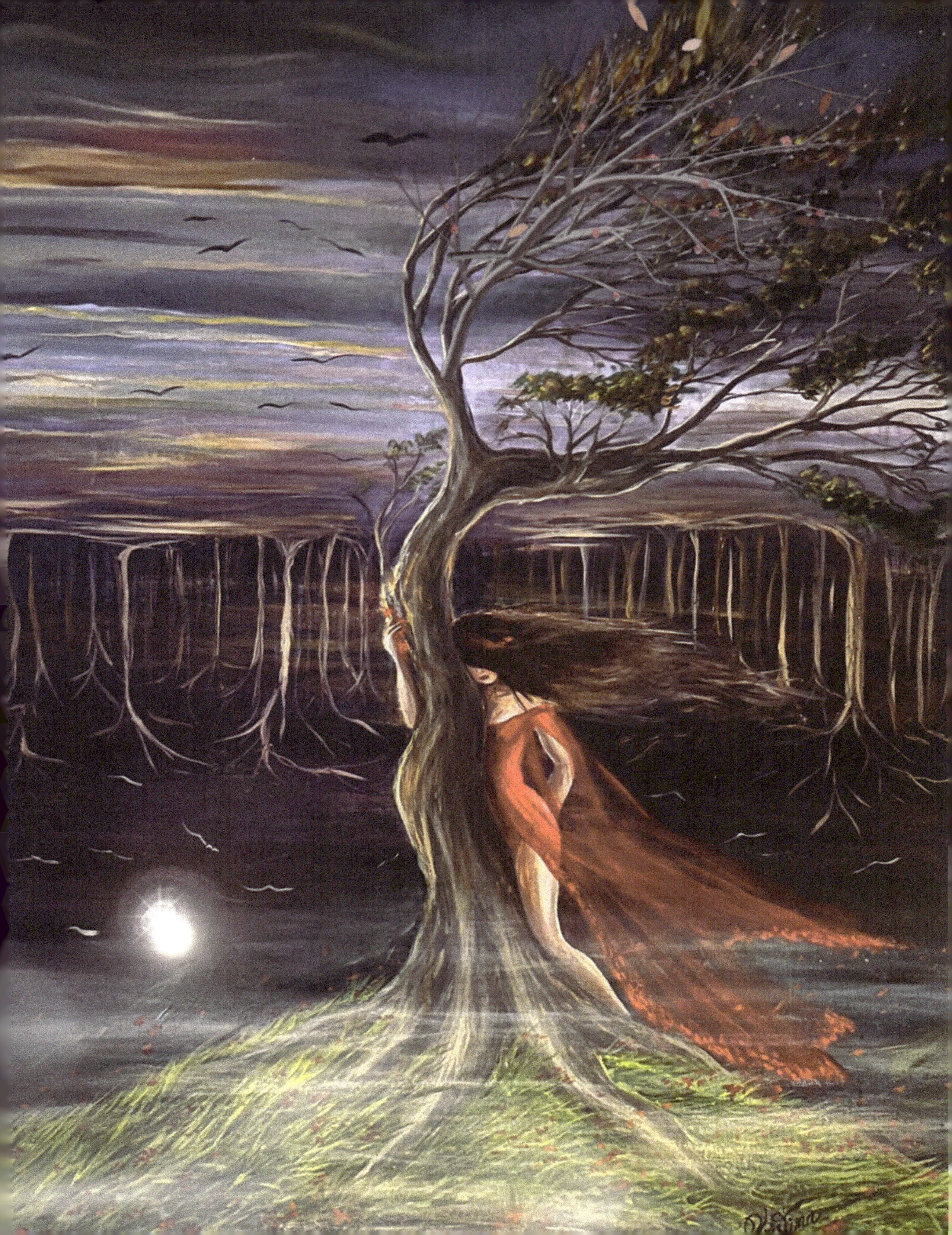

Sunrays

My heart has sunken in my chest. I am in so much pain!

But right now, as I write this, gray cloudy skies crack open, and the warm golden light of the sun has descended through my window to caress my face.

I needed that.

I needed a reminder that in the midst of my heartache, in these murky moments of my life, the light of the Almighty – the-Creator-of-all-things, embraces and illuminates me in my brokenness.

Abba Father, please hold me in your arms.

For in my weakness Your love is my strength.

Gratitude

Today, I thank God for Ari's life. For the years He loaned her to us.

I am grateful for the six years granted after the first cancer diagnosis.

I am thankful I was chosen to be her mother.

Though no longer with me physically, my child is with me in unexplainable ways for always.

I give thanks for the good and the bad.

For the darkness and the light.

I was bitter for a time. I was mad at God, at life, at the entire universe.

He was not shaken by my humanity or by my descent into grief.

He knew I would be distraught, shocked, furious, but most of all, broken beyond recognition.

I now know He was there all along.

And,

He still loved me through it all.

Time and time again, I became lost in the tsunamic tides of pain that threatened to drown me. Like a battered ship, I have sunken in these dark waters many times.

But I have not perished. I am here still. I have resurfaced above those murky waters. And that means my work here is not done yet.

Through the years, a slow healing process has taken place.

An organic progression that at times entailed putting together the puzzle I had become.

I was crushed, and pieces of myself splattered everywhere.

I selected the shards of myself that enabled me to function in life. I hid the rest in the depths of my being.

Time has taught me that those hidden pieces, that unresolved grief, actually festers when not dealt with, when not allowed to heal.

I'm arriving to a point I thought would never come.

Gradually, I have begun to face pain in its totality.

Finally, I am allowing God to fill in the gaping holes of my fragmented self with His love and grace, His strength and His mercy.

This integration process has not been a smooth sail.

I find myself in the midst of an ongoing metamorphosis.

I am learning to slow down and to appreciate the new image of me that has begun to unfold. To love the woman I am becoming, this different version of myself.

I am grateful for the work in progress that I am.

The experience of losing my child sprang forth profound lessons. Teachings that change my priorities in life. Learnings that altered me forever.

In this life nothing goes to waste – especially the lessons learned during hardship.

God uses all of it for good, even this terrible loss.

I know I will stumble and fall. But I also know that even when I can't hold on to the One above, He holds me tight and raises me up.

I am thankful for the glimpses of eternity I have experienced even thought I do not deserve them.

I am so grateful for the certainty that my child is alive and well; living on the other side of the thin veil that separate this side of heaven from hers.

I know that one day I will be with her again.

But until then,

I will choose to open my eyes to the goodness that still surrounds me, to love deeply and to continue in the process of becoming what I am meant to be in this life.

I will navigate the currents of my grieving process for as long as it takes.

But in the course, I will allow myself to learn to use this undying love to overcome my pain, and to overcome my darkness.

With God's help, I might be able to shed light into another's shadowy path.

I will choose gratitude as much as I possibly can!

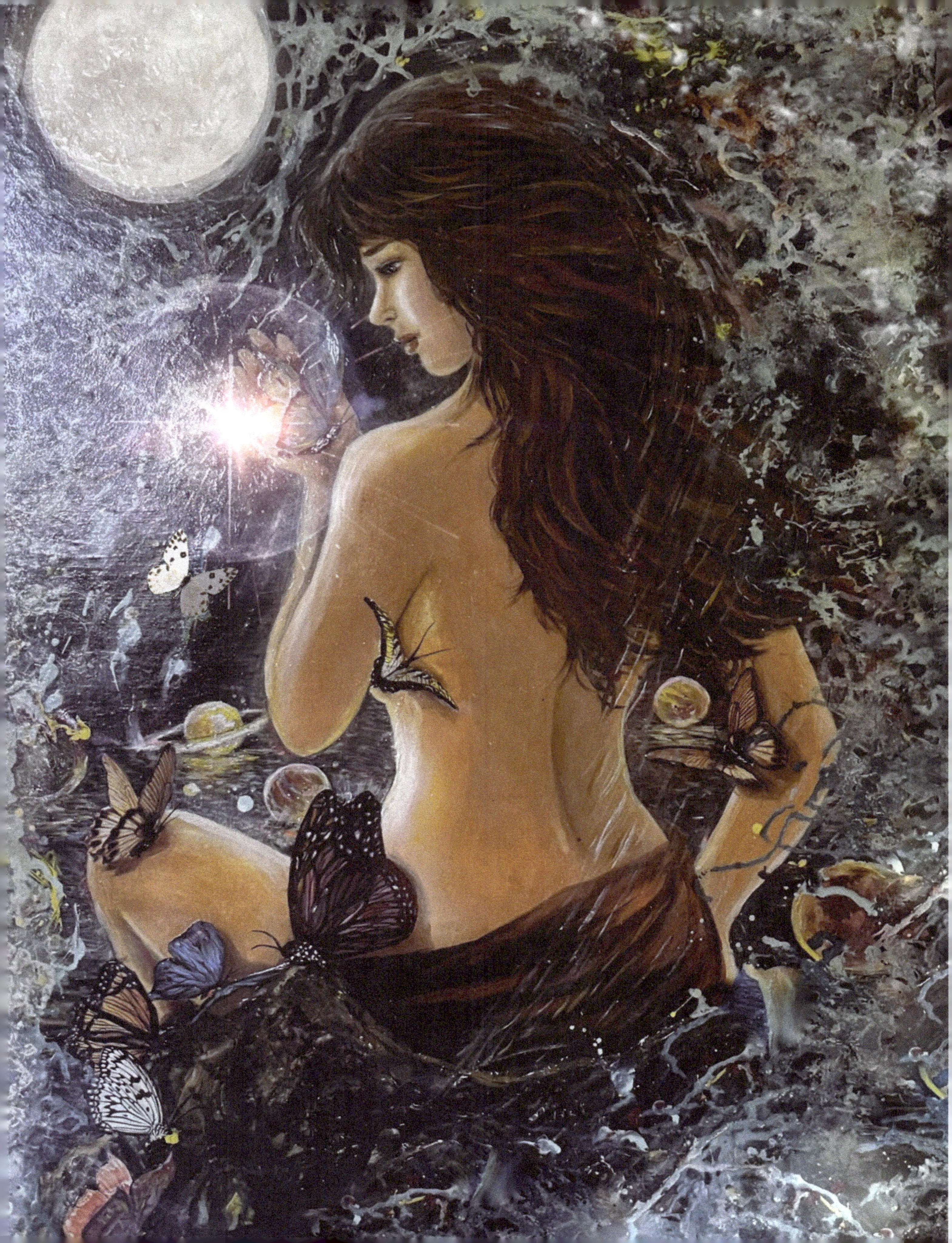

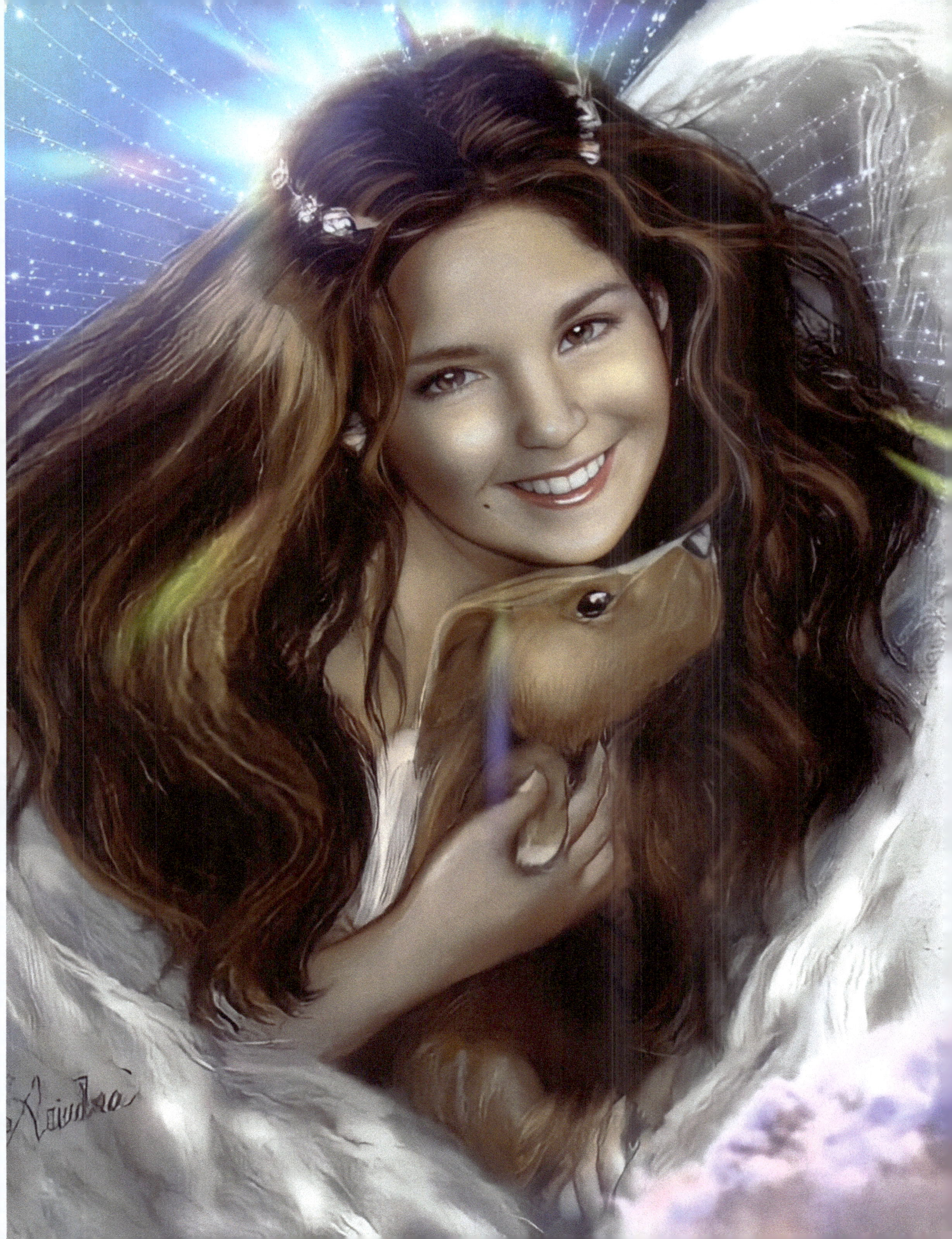

The Child

Who went to Heaven

Her voice set me free
With her voice,
my mom let go of me

Then, into the air, I rose
I pierced the veil that separates us from immortality
To immensity I am guided
Fluttering I go in this warm and serene light
Enveloped I go in my angel's protection

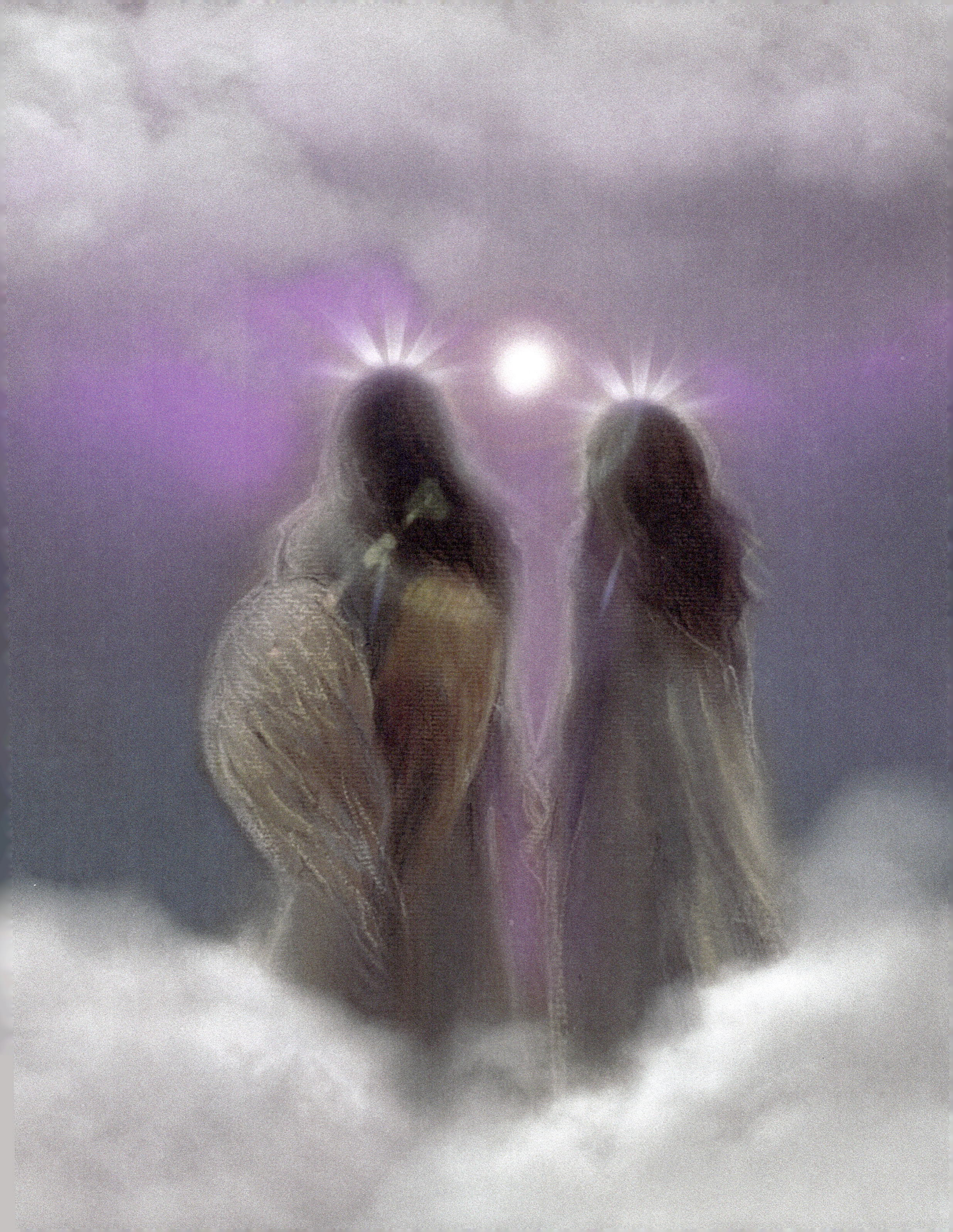

Beyond the stars that illuminate the dark vault of the night
Farther away from the sun, I fly
The Milky Way and other constellations, in a flash, I pass by

Far away we go
Away we go from where all my human body and senses had imprisoned me
Farther still we go
We are crossing universes and dimensions
Now I am without flaws and limitations

I now live beyond human wisdom
Beyond its comprehension,
I am alive!

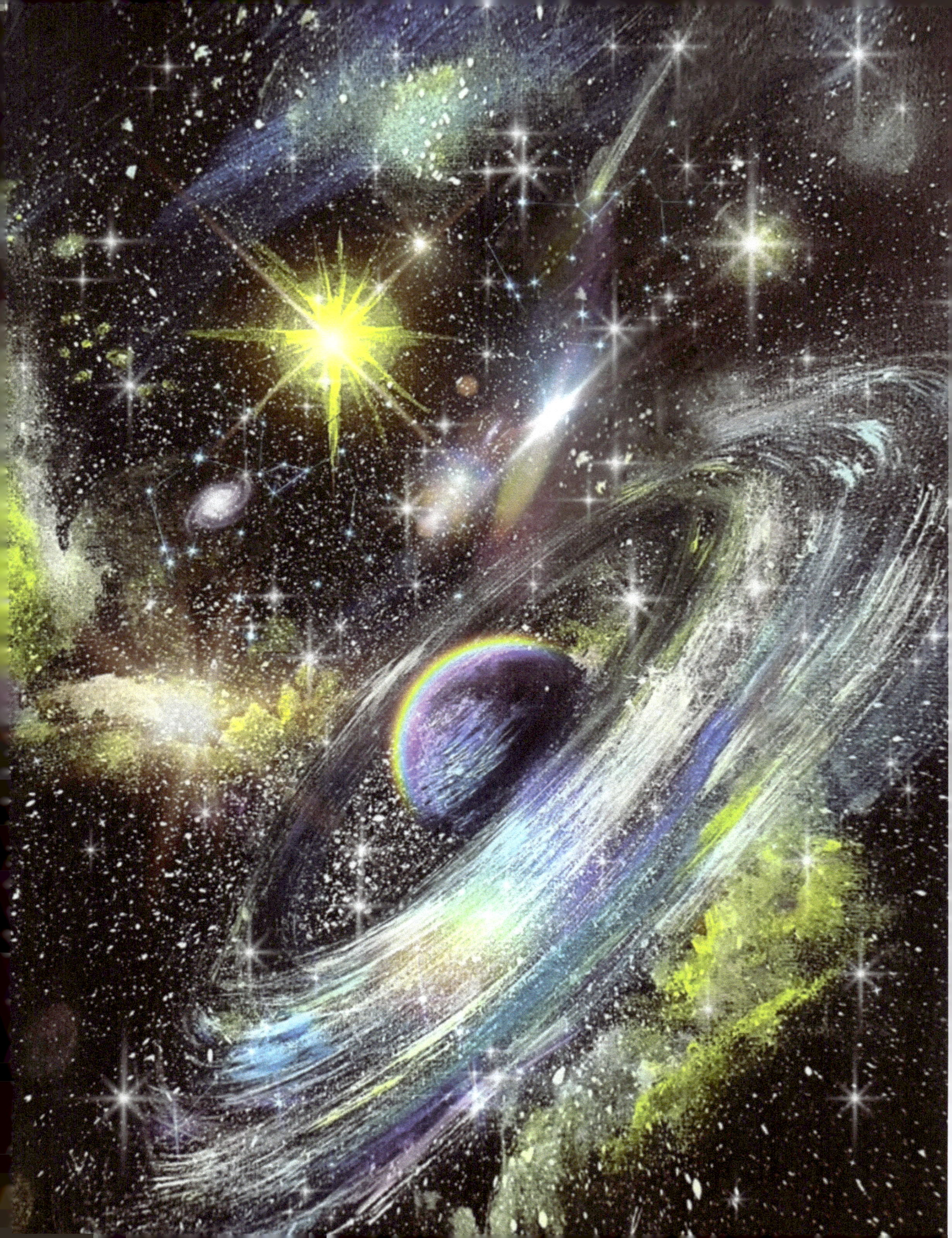

For a moment I look back
And on my face a fleeting smile is drawn

I come bursting of love
Of goodness that overflows
and of wisdom
Clothed in light I come

Ineradicable are the learnings
of my experiences from that life

A blink of an eye is a life time on Earth
Short or long, a flicker, tiny in breadth

Life does not end there
It simply transforms
It continues to grow
I am ready for what is to come

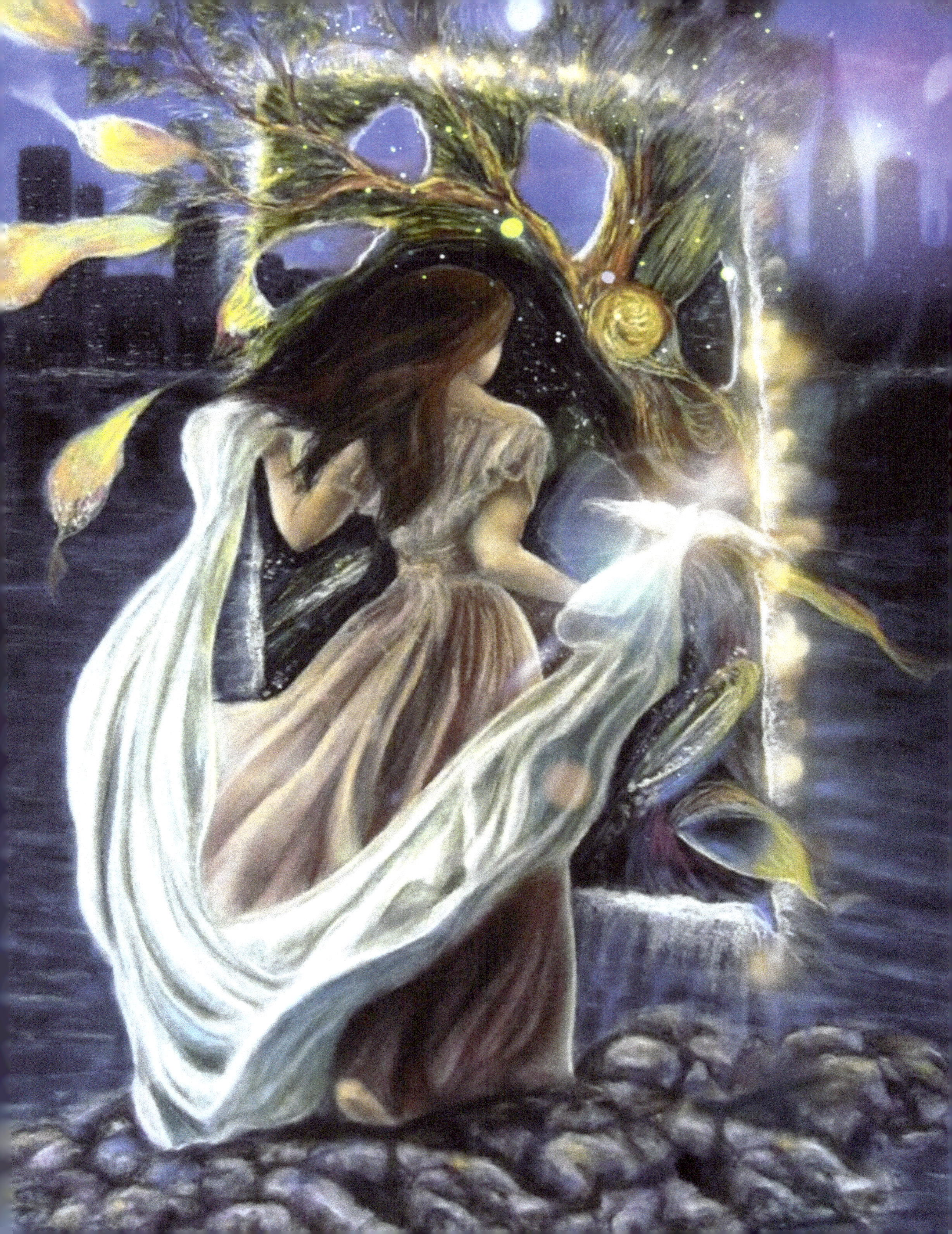

Attired I go in all that I am now
Hundreds have come
They encircle me in their light
They embrace me in their love

So much laughter and joy,
Together we glow!

Beaming I let go of them for a moment
I turn to continue my journey

The awaited re-encounter with my Creator
The One Who Was, The One Who Is, The One Who Will Be
Indescribable is His glory
Unmeasurable is His love
Into His arms I surrender
His loving embrace I now remember

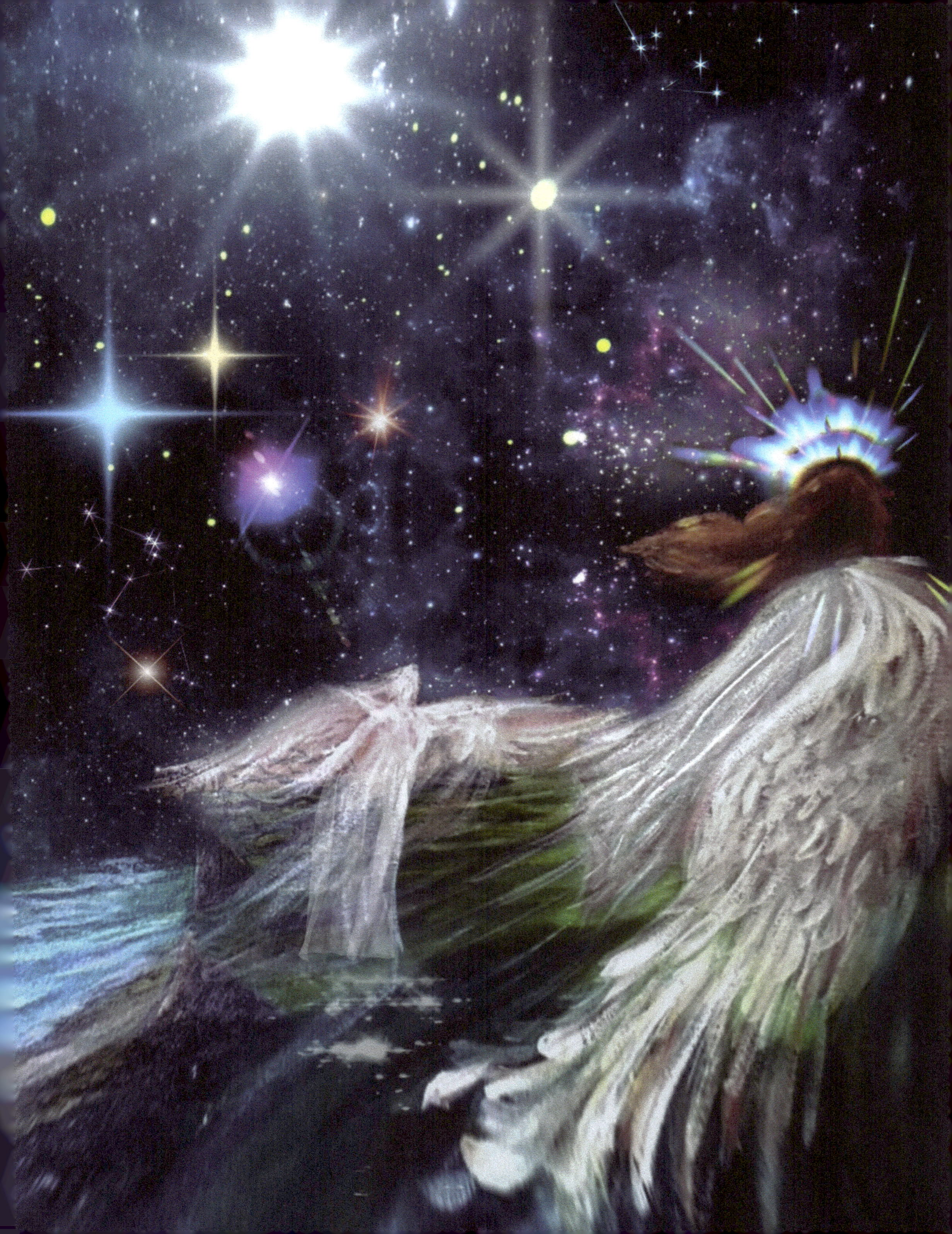

There are no words that can describe
the amount of joy that in my heart resides
In the light of exaltation, I ascend
Bathed in stars I dance for Him
To Him, in adoration I sing

To my surprise I hear my voice
as it widens in angelic high frequencies
sound waves that take artful shapes and colorful forms

I smile and the whole of the Heavens rejoices with me
Full of delight we celebrate

And then,
one by one,
the rest of my loved ones have finally arrived

Reunited in eternity,
together in our celestial home
with our Lord we shall forever remain.
There are no words that could explain
For no human words could ever convey
For nothing on earth can be compared
To the glorious life we found in Him!

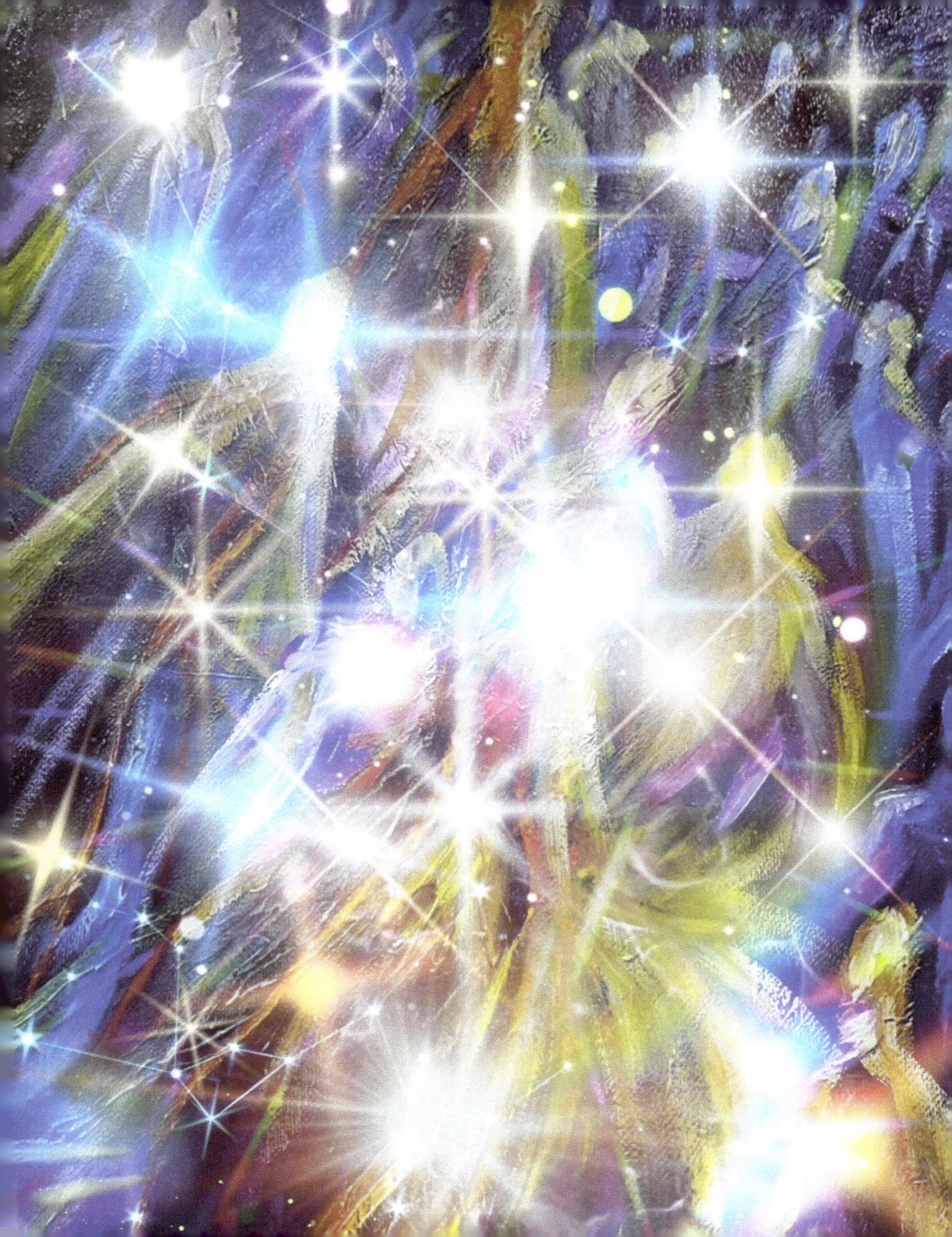

About the Author and Illustrator

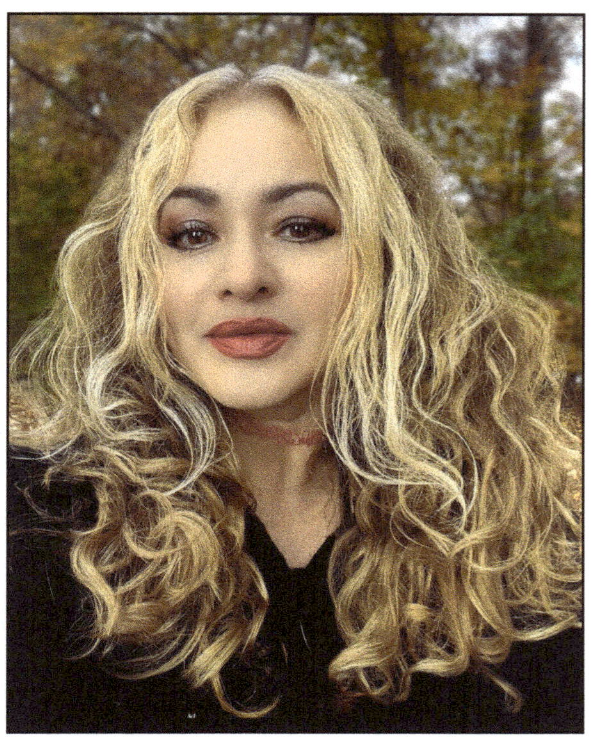

Kristina is a Fine Art artist, sculptor, writer, educator, and illustrator. Born in Paradisiacal, Costa Rica, she studied Law at the University of Costa Rica.

Today, as a proud citizen of the United States, she has successfully parlayed her love and passion for the arts into two entities: *Kristina's Fine Art* and *Artistic Kreations with Kristina*. She has made it her mission in life to share the wonder found within the creation of art with her students or with whomever may take time to listen!

In her own words .... "As a Fine Artist, each original art piece is a bridge by which I can liberate my soul and spirit from the vast emotions transmitted through me. My paintings are a spontaneous response to my inner voice, always striving to capture the essence of humanity, nature, and matters of Faith."

As an illustrator, she often returns to her inner child. It is that child that takes over – conveying wonder and emotions to be able to tell stories and tales full of color and beauty.

As a writer, she approaches each story with a deep reverence, as each original work is like a vision that will never be revealed in the same way again.

Kristina's artworks have been exhibited in Miami, FL; Atlanta, GA; Chattanooga, TN; Costa Rica; Italy and Spain and collected by private art collectors worldwide. She has illustrated books for authors in the USA, Spain, Portugal, Ivory Coast and Italy.

She is a published author with multiple literary and illustrative contributions in international anthologies for the *Biblioteca de las Grandes Naciones* based in the Basque Country of Spain.

Kristina has a deep love and passion for the community which she has served over the years in many different capacities. She was awarded the La Paz, Latino Leader of the year.

Stay tuned for upcoming books from Kristina!
For more information visit **https://www.kristinasfineart.com/**
Follow her on
Facebook: Of Loss, Grief and Hope
Facebook: Kristina's Fine Art
Instagram: kristina_sanchez_mills_
TikTok: @krysunica

Warnock Pro and Bickham Script Pro on 70# LSI archival white
Type and design by Karen Paul Stone

www.ingramcontent.com/pod-product-compliance
Lightning Source LLC
LaVergne TN
LVHW060620110826
345147LV00019B/1059
* 9 7 8 1 9 4 7 5 8 9 7 0 4 *